PENGUIN BOOKS

I ACCUSE . . .

Jarnail Singh was born in Delhi in 1973. After a master's degree in political science from PGDAV College, he completed a diploma in journalism from the YMCA in 1994. He was special correspondent with *Dainik Jagran*, Delhi, for ten years, covering the fields of Sikh politics and defence. He has written extensively on the Sikh massacre of 1984 and its aftermath. He lives with his wife and two children in New Delhi.

PENGUIN BOOKS

[illegible]

[illegible] was born in Delhi in 19[illegible]. [illegible] degree in political science [illegible] College. He completed a diploma in journalism from the YMCA in 19[illegible]. He was [illegible] correspondent with [illegible] [illegible] [illegible] [illegible] with his wife and two children in New Delhi.

I ACCUSE . . .

The Anti-Sikh Violence of 1984

JARNAIL SINGH

With a Foreword by
Khushwant Singh

PENGUIN BOOKS

PENGUIN BOOKS
Published by the Penguin Group
Penguin Books India Pvt. Ltd, 11 Community Centre, Panchsheel Park, New Delhi 110 017, India
Penguin Group (USA) Inc., 375 Hudson Street, New York, New York 10014, USA
Penguin Group (Canada), 90 Eglinton Avenue East, Suite 700, Toronto, Ontario, M4P 2Y3, Canada (a division of Pearson Penguin Canada Inc.)
Penguin Books Ltd, 80 Strand, London WC2R 0RL, England
Penguin Ireland, 25 St Stephen's Green, Dublin 2, Ireland (a division of Penguin Books Ltd)
Penguin Group (Australia), 250 Camberwell Road, Camberwell, Victoria 3124, Australia (a division of Pearson Australia Group Pty Ltd)
Penguin Group (NZ), 67 Apollo Drive, Rosedale, Auckland 0632, New Zealand
Penguin Group (South Africa) (Pty) Ltd, 24 Sturdee Avenue, Rosebank, Johannesburg 2196, South Africa

Penguin Books Ltd, Registered Offices: 80 Strand, London WC2R 0RL, England

First published in Viking by Penguin Books India 2009
Published in Penguin Books 2011

Copyright © Jarnail Singh 2009

Translated from the Hindi by Vaishali Mathur

All rights reserved

10 9 8 7 6 5 4 3 2

The views and opinions expressed in this book are the author's own and the facts are as reported by him, which have been verified to the extent possible, and the publishers are not in any way liable for the same.

ISBN 9780143417521

Typeset in Dante MT by InoSoft Systems, Noida
Printed at Chaman Offset Printers, Delhi

This book is sold subject to the condition that it shall not, by way of trade or otherwise, be lent, resold, hired out, or otherwise circulated without the publisher's prior written consent in any form of binding or cover other than that in which it is published and without a similar condition including this condition being imposed on the subsequent purchaser and without limiting the rights under copyright reserved above, no part of this publication may be reproduced, stored in or introduced into a retrieval system, or transmitted in any form or by any means (electronic, mechanical, photocopying, recording or otherwise), without the prior written permission of both the copyright owner and the above-mentioned publisher of this book.

This book is dedicated to all the victims of the Sikh massacre of 1984

It is a crime to lie to the public, to twist public opinion to insane lengths in the service of the vilest death-dealing machinations. It is a crime to poison the minds of the meek and the humble, to stoke the passions of reactionism and intolerance . . . It is a crime to exploit patriotism in the service of hatred, and it is, finally, a crime to ensconce the sword as the modern god . . .

Truth and justice, so ardently longed for! How terrible it is to see them trampled, unrecognized and ignored!

—Émile Zola, 'I Accuse'
Letter to the President of the French Republic, 1898

[Émile Zola, the eminent French novelist, wrote an impassioned appeal entitled 'I Accuse' in defence of Captain Alfred Dreyfus who was falsely accused of treason and sentenced to penal servitude. Zola pointed to the underlying anti-Semitism in the case against Dreyfus, the fabrication of evidence and the cover-up by France's military establishment. The case divided French society but eventually Dreyfus was retried and acquitted. 'J'accuse' became an iconic expression of how citizens can fight injustice and win.]

Contents

Foreword

Jarnail Singh's *I Accuse . . .* is a shocking book that should shame every citizen of India. It is a searing account of the brutal massacre of Sikhs in Delhi and other parts of north India following the assassination of Mrs Gandhi by two of her Sikh bodyguards. It is also a scathing indictment of the people who planned and perpetrated the massacre and of those in power who displayed criminal indifference to the widespread killing and destruction of property.

This includes the then president Giani Zail Singh who shrugged off his responsibility as head of state and Narasimha Rao who abdicated his responsibility to restore law and order as the country's home minister. The book is also unsparing in its description of the role played in the killings by lackeys of the Congress Party, many of whom, including H.K.L. Bhagat, Dharam Dass Shastri, Jagdish Tytler and Sajjan Kumar, according to many testimonies, which I fully believe, took active part by leading mobs of hooligans to attack gurdwaras and Sikh localities. Far from being punished for their actions, they were rewarded by Prime Minister Rajiv Gandhi by being accommodated in his cabinet of ministers. He himself exonerated the killers of innocent people in his first public speech after he took over as prime minister, by saying, 'But when a mighty tree falls, it is only natural that the earth around it does shake a little.' It is a long tale of injustice which rankles in one's mind to this day.

Jarnail Singh picked on the wrong man to hurl his shoe at. P.C. Chidambaram had nothing whatsoever to do with the pogrom of 1984. However the shoe missed its target and that is just as well since Jarnail Singh has said repeatedly, as he does in this book, that it was an emotional reaction which he is not proud of. But it roused people's conscience against the patronage extended by the Congress Party to men like Tytler and Sajjan Kumar, both of whom were again picked as the party's candidates in the Lok Sabha elections. Jarnail Singh's action at least ensured that they were dropped by the Congress from its final list of candidates. However, those responsible for the massacre still need to be brought to justice.

I Accuse . . . opens wounds which have not yet healed. It is a must-read for all those who wish that such horrendous crimes do not take place again.

New Delhi — Khushwant Singh
September 2009

ONE

31 October 1984

'I did not even know who Indira was. I had neither read a newspaper, nor watched TV. By the evening of 31 October some people—many from the nearby basti—started forcing their way into Sikh houses and taking away TVs and fridges. When a few of them tried to come towards us, Sardarji took out his kirpan and chased them away. I could hear faint cries of "Burn them. Don't leave Sikhs alive". I told my husband, "Chalo ji, let's go somewhere else," but he gave me a good scolding. He said "How can they kill anybody like this? Isn't there something called the law?"

'I could not sleep all night. Next day we got up early to find that it was quiet everywhere. I was bathing my one-year-old son, Ladi, when suddenly a huge crowd turned up. I could only see heads outside. The mob bought kerosene from a nearby shop, dipped sacks in it and set them alight. They threw the burning sacks inside the house. When the house started burning we had no choice but to rush out . . . a brick thrown by the crowd hit Sardarji on the head and he fell, bleeding profusely. I tied my scarf around his head and took him inside, locking the door. The mob was banging on the door saying bring Sardarji out. I went on to the veranda and put my three children in front of them and begged for mercy. They did not have any pity. Then

they changed their tune and said almost politely, "You people go to Punjab and we will not do anything." I had no idea then that some of them had climbed on to the roof. I began taking Sardarji outside when one jumped from the roof and hit him with a rod. Blood poured out. I took Sardarji's head in my hands and started begging. But they were beyond listening—they hit him again and again with sticks and iron rods. I too received a few blows—even today my hand still hurts. The house was set on fire again and I pulled out the children and Sardarji to the street. What could I have done? Our home was burning. None come forward to help, though I begged and begged. There was no way to take Sardarji to either the hospital or the doctor. The crowd had gathered around and was watching. I was tearing off bits from my dupatta and trying to staunch the wounds. They threw kerosene and some sort of inflammable white powder over me and Sardarji. One of them said, "This bloody woman has not left him since morning. Burn both of them." They were about to light the match when somebody from the nearby Hindu priest's house stepped in and said that they would not allow them to say or do anything to women and children. But it was clear to the mob that they could burn Sardarji. I have no idea if the priests did the right thing or not. Sometimes I feel that it was a good thing that they saved my honour from the mob but sometimes I think that if the mob was listening so much to the priests, then they should have saved Sardarji too. I don't know how Sardarji must have died. I was sobbing when I was pulled away from there. He would have probably survived the pain of his wounds but the rioters had thrown kerosene and white powder over him. They must have burnt him alive.'

Before Partition my grandfather used to live in a village close to Lahore. When he came to India, he came empty-handed and was allotted a house in Lajpat Nagar that had a tin roof which made it very cold in winter and very hot in summer. But my parents felt that at least it was a home. The roof abutted the neighbouring house and it was possible to reach every house nearby by simply climbing on to it.

My father got a job as a carpenter, and with that a regular income started to come in. As time went by, we improved the house and it felt like a home. Our family was a large one—I have five brothers and three sisters. When we were growing up, we would roam around Lajpat Nagar the whole day and it never worried my mother.

Lajpat Nagar was a refugee colony for the Hindus and Sikhs who had come from Pakistan after Partition. They all shared the same experiences of pain and separation which gave a sense of common purpose—no one felt alienated here. One of our neighbours was an elderly lady called 'Bhabhiji' by everyone. She was from Multan and was especially close to my mother. In fact, after Bhabhiji died, her daughter-in-law treated my mother like her mother-in-law, as that is what Bhabhiji would have wanted. Some years ago when Bhabhiji's grandchildren got married, my mother took on the role of the grandmother-in-law though Bhabhiji had been a Hindu and my mother was a Sikh.

It had never mattered. But on this day, 31 October 1984, there were those who wanted all such relationships to be severed. Bhabhiji came to the house several times that day. 'Don't worry,' she said in Multani, but she clearly didn't believe her own words. Rumours were rife in the neighbourhood that after Mrs Gandhi's assassination at the hands of her Sikh bodyguards, mobs were attacking Sikhs in several areas of the city. But in quiet Lajpat Nagar on the afternoon of 31 October, that seemed distant, even if worrying. Nonetheless, Mother removed our father's nameplate from outside the house and warned Bhabhiji not to come too often for her own safety. Ours was the only Sikh house in the entire lane, though there were others across the nallah.

At home the worry lines on Papa's face were apparent. In the evening my aunt, who lived in Arjun Nagar near

Safdarjung Enclave, called and related an incident about her Sikh neighbour. He had been crossing the road at the All India Institute of Medical Science (AIIMS) when he saw an angry mob pulling Sikhs out of their vehicles and beating them up; their pagris were being torn off. He himself had escaped by a whisker. We heard that President Giani Zail Singh had gone to AIIMS to pay his respects to the slain prime minister and the mob threw stones at his cavalcade. When Mother came back after taking my aunt's call in the neighbouring house of Kabul Singh (we did not have a telephone), she looked very uneasy. However, no one could imagine then what was to take place the next day. Since Indira Gandhi was the prime minister, national mourning had been declared. Radio and television (only AIR and Doordarshan in those days) were only broadcasting mournful veena music. We kids were not happy with this at all. Mourning was for grown-ups; as far as we children were concerned it was a holiday and we wanted to see the normal programmes on television.

On 1 November, early in the morning, we went out to play cricket in the nearby Shiv Vatika park with our friends from the neighbourhood. This park was to one side of the colony and we would play for hours—unchecked and unaware. It was only when we got tired that we would remember we had homes. This was entirely usual—we would be so engrossed in the game that we would forgot that we had not eaten and would return only to be scolded by our mothers who would say, 'Why! You didn't find a mother in the park to feed you? Stay there!' We knew they weren't really angry. But today was different.

We had just reached the Sindhi school when we heard shouts and raised voices. A crowd was screaming. We looked at each other and decided that we would investigate further—I suppose all kids would have the same reaction. We were curious—and till then we'd had nothing to fear. However, just then my elder brother, who was thirteen years old at that time, said, 'Do you want to get scolded by Mother? Let's go straight home, we haven't even had breakfast this morning.' He was the strongest amongst us and generally no one opposed him. We had just reached our lane when we saw that Mother was standing outside the house, looking frantic with worry. I still remember the scolding that we got that day. She even slapped us once or twice. Mother was extremely worked up and the relief of seeing the three of us safe and sound somehow made her angrier. A neighbour's son, Raju, had actually been sent to look for us. He had searched the parks nearby but could not find us as the Shiv Vatika park was a little distance away. When we could not be traced for a long time, Mother became frantic. Even so, my brothers and I could not understand why she was so scared.

Before we could ask any questions, my two brothers and I were locked up in a room right in the back of the house. Its door had not been closed in a long time so it was difficult to lock. Father used all his force and shut it tight. We could not understand why all this was happening, but we realized that whatever it was, it was serious. Satvinder Kaur, my eldest sister, told us that there was some looting and Sikhs were being beaten up. This was the first time I had heard the word 'loot'. Curious, I watched from the window: Mother was now washing clothes but clearly also keeping a watch on events in the street.

When the noise of the mob began to get louder, Mother told us to climb up to the 'oltee', the small space at the head of the staircase, and hide there. Usually we only went up there while playing hide-and-seek—and we were always scolded for it; but today we were actually being told to do so. For a long time my two brothers and I—we were then thirteen, eleven and ten years old—crouched in that dark, cramped place. My elder brother, Jasbir Singh, had been sent off to a neighbour's house—Mother had heard that adolescent boys were being especially targeted and she felt he'd be safer out of our house. It was suffocating up in the attic. Mother had been too distracted to give us any food and we had not even had our breakfast that morning—we'd run off to play cricket without eating anything. We were famished till we found a large tin box full of wheat flour biscuits from Chander bakery. Mother had got them made planning to give us a couple every day on winter mornings as atta was said to keep you warm. This tin was stored in the oltee. We finished almost the whole box—I can still remember how good they tasted. We were so young, so unscarred then. It never occurred to us to wonder why we had to hide like criminals in our own house inside a colony we had lived in all our lives, surrounded by neighbours with whom we'd always had good relations. How could this have happened? Even today, I don't know. While we were still locked up there, Bhabhiji had turned up again. She told Mother that the gurdwara had been set on fire and Sikh shops in the nearby Krishna Market were being looted and set ablaze. Bhabhiji had just seen a neighbour's son carrying boxes of shoes out of the looted shops. He had picked up twenty pairs for himself from the Central Market shop Volga which belonged to a Sardar. It is a different thing that he found he had stolen twenty pairs of the same type of shoe. He was an exception. Most of our neighbours in the colony did not participate in the mob frenzy; but they did not do anything to stop it. Nor did they actively get together with the looters and plunderers, though some boys seized the opportunity to pick up things.

We were taken out of the room late in the night. Then our eldest brother, Gurcharan, who had a bad leg due to a childhood attack of polio, decided to go to Niwaspuri. Our father had recently been allotted a government quarter in Niwaspuri as he was in the Central Public Works Department (CPWD) and Gurcharan was staying there as it was near his college. Despite being plagued by polio he had been studying hard and after completing his B.Com. he was planning to study further to become a company secretary. People at home told him not to leave the house because the situation was not good. He dismissed their warnings: 'I am disabled and going on a tricycle, who will say anything to me?' His confidence in the kindness of strangers was misplaced that day: 1 November 1984. He was attacked a short distance from the house. His three-wheeled cycle was overturned. His pagri was pulled off and the mob started beating him, heedless of his cries of pain. His disability made it impossible for him to run. He was lying in the dust, while the blows rained down on him. The mob left him bleeding and shaken on the road. A few shopkeepers, who knew him but hadn't intervened when he was actually being beaten up, came forward once the mob had left. They put the cycle straight and helped him back on it. He came home somehow but for a long time he was in a state of shock. He had always been treated with consideration. That day he learnt that the only thing that mattered was that he was a Sikh.

We spent the entire day taking God's name. The next day, 2 November, Mother looked even more worried. Our aunt had called up with some shocking news. Mother's younger brother, our uncle, Gulzar Singh, and other Sikh drivers had been attacked by the mob at the Hyatt Regency hotel's taxi stand. Mama, our uncle, used to run his taxi there, a taxi bought with the money saved by our maternal grandfather when he had worked in Baluchistan before Partition. The mob had beaten up all the Sikh taxi drivers at the rank very badly, leaving them bleeding and bruised, their clothes covered with blood. They had been left for dead. Uncle was a strapping young man. If there had been only five or even ten against him, he could have tackled them alone. But the attackers ran into hundreds.

Despite his severe injuries, we had learnt that it was useless to take him to a government hospital. AIIMS was the nearest hospital, but news had spread that President Zail Singh's motor cavalcade had been attacked by angry mobs when he had come to the hospital to pay his respects to the slain prime minister. If that was the treatment meted out to the head of state, what hope did ordinary Sikhs have. Government hospitals were not admitting injured Sikhs; we heard that such hospitals had actually closed their burns unit—so that the many Sikhs who had been set ablaze by the mobs were unable to get the treatment that they so desperately needed.

One of the most inhuman acts of the mobs was to fit car tyres over their victims' heads and then set the tyres alight. There were many Sikhs with burn injuries, but even if a victim managed to reach a government hospital, he would have been turned back. In fact, several Sikhs who were turned away from hospitals fell victim to mobs on their way home. My uncle, despite his injuries, had to be kept at home. My aunt could not find a doctor to treat him—many were too scared to go to the house of a Sikh, fearing retribution from the mobs. A private nurse—a Christian—who lived nearby, agreed to come every day and dress the wounds. It was such gestures—the courage and compassion of strangers—that no one who has been through those days can forget.

That day, 2 November, a police jeep went around the colony announcing that a curfew would be imposed within half an hour. They advised everyone to stay home.

Mother was relieved. 'Everything will be okay now,' she said; after all, the mobs could not gather to attack during a curfew. But the curfew was not implemented. Anyone who breaks a curfew is liable to be shot at sight, or at least apprehended. But from what I saw on 2 November, no sooner had the jeep announcing curfew passed by than more and more people would spill out of their homes. People told me later that local Congressmen were responsible for the attacks on the Sikhs of Lajpat Nagar. Some even alleged that the two sons of a local leader were seen brandishing the voters' list, so that the mobs could be directed to Sikh houses. The Hindus in our neighbourhood decided to set up patrols at night so that they could protect their lives and property.

This patrol was set up close to our house and all the people on it were from our neighbourhood, so I knew them all. Escaping from my mother, I reached the spot where they had gathered. That is when I came to know that our non-Sikh neighbours were also scared. Rumours were rife that to avenge Sikh killings a trainload of Sikhs were coming from Punjab ready to attack innocent Hindus and that many Hindus were being killed in Punjab. Another rumour, also widespread, was that the Sikhs had mixed poison in the city's drinking water supply. I actually asked someone how he thought this was possible and he pointed to the reservoir which supplied water to Lajpat Nagar. But even I, a child at the time, knew immediately this was ridiculous. In the first place, who could climb such a huge tank? And if they had managed to poison the water, wouldn't the water flow to Sikh houses too? But it was such a strong rumour that I half believed it too. I had just drunk some water at home and I was scared—this is how the disinformation was working. The purpose of the rumour was to make everyone believe that the Sikhs were on a rampage, to incite public opinion against them, to quell any sympathy that might be developing for them because of the mobs' killing spree.

We didn't know then the extent of the horror that had taken place. Reports in the newspapers were few; but our family and friends would hear about the violence from *their* families and friends. The stories we heard were unbelievable; but we had to believe them. We had seen the spires of black smoke from burning taxi stands from our roof; we had heard about innocent Sikhs being brutally beaten; accounts of the massacres in Kalyanpuri and Trilokpuri were beginning to come out. All this was frightening, because no one knew why this had happened; who was behind it. Shock and worry had gripped my parents; my brothers and I were scared as well, but we were children and we did not really understand the full extent of the violence.

After ten days when life began returning to normal we were allowed to go and play in the park again. We were tired of staying home. The park was our life. All three of us went to play and we found the other kids in the park were in the middle of a game of touchball—where you have to hit the other players with the ball. The ball used to cost just fifty paise but the hits really hurt. The three of us took a while to realize that we were being hit the hardest and most often. It dawned on us that the other boys were making us targets. It was not a game; it was a form of making us scapegoats. None of the other children were being treated that way. The balls thrown at them were ones they could catch easily; the ball wasn't being thrown at them with the intention to hurt. Perhaps we should have just stopped playing—but we were children too. We were not in the habit of running away. Swiftly, the three of us targeted the others, one by one. It was a war, not a game. The hits were painful, but we three pretended they didn't hurt. We didn't stop playing with the kids in the park—we had played with them all our lives. But that day we all realized that the question of being a Hindu or a Sikh had entered even children's games.

We were all in the same age group and went to the same school. We spent our free time together and plucked Ramchandra Aunty's and Roshini Aunty's guavas together. We used to fight earlier too but now we became the objects of taunts, 'Sardaron ke barah baj gaye,' they would shout. They'd said this to us before, but this was different; this was not a joke, but a taunt. One of the boys, Titu we called him, said, 'If you fight too much, I will call the same people who killed Sikhs on 31 October and 1 November. Your house got saved in the riots but this time I will tell them the correct address.' Titu was in my class, his mother and my mother were friends. Children have fights, it's natural; but it was also natural that we started reacting aggressively too. Today I am still friends with many of those boys; we don't speak of that time. When I was younger, I thought I would forget. I know now that things will never be the same again.

There are still people who feel the Sikhs brought the horror of 1984 upon themselves. They justify the pogrom by talking of the acts of terror that had been committed by some individuals who called themselves Sikhs. What civilized society tolerates this kind of logic?

There is no place for terrorism in any society. It should be condemned in the strongest possible way. The killing of journalists, of the passengers pulled out of buses and the transistor bomb explosions in Delhi and other places shocked me to the core, even though I was still a young schoolboy when they took place. I felt then, as I do now, that those who indulged in such actions were not true Sikhs, for it is completely against the Sikh faith to harm innocent people. But to me there is also no difference between such acts of terror and the state-sponsored terrorism that was the massacre of Sikhs in 1984.

The chain of events that led to the carnage of 1984 had been a long time in the making. I was eleven years old when Operation Blue Star took place and while I have some memories of it, I could not then fathom the intricacies behind it. Later as a journalist I covered Punjab and Sikh politics continuously, and it was then that I looked at the history and tried to understand what had led to such events.

In the decades since Independence, tensions had surfaced in the previously impregnable Sikh–Hindu brotherhood. The Punjabi Suba issue, the allocation of Chandigarh, the river waters issue—among others—had led to schisms which were exploited by all the major parties in order to gain political mileage. Many in the Sikh community felt betrayed: the Sikh contribution to not just the freedom struggle, but to all the wars that Independent India had fought—as well as to the prosperity of the country—was unquestioned. But the situation between New Delhi and

Punjab deteriorated to such an extent that the late seventies and early eighties witnessed the raising of the separatist slogan of 'Khalistan' and the formation of groups that used violent means to gain their ends. The centre reacted by clamping down relentlessly through staged encounters, raising the spectre of the break up of the country and routinely projecting all Sikhs as terrorists.

The stage had been set for Operation Blue Star. The then deputy army chief, Lt General S.K. Sinha, was slated for the army's top job when Lt General A.S. Vaidya was appointed at the last minute. Lt General Sinha has attributed this move to his refusal to attack the Golden Temple. According to Sinha, the plan to attack the Golden Temple was being formulated for a year-and-a-half before the final assault and in preparation the army had been planning the attack using a model of the Golden Temple in the Chakrata area near Dehra Dun. If this is true, it points towards a very deep conspiracy. The question here is also that why was the day of Guru Arjun Dev's martyrdom chosen for the attack? On this day the gathering of devotees is many times that of a normal day. The action resulted in the death of 5,000 innocent Sikh pilgrims, leading to a widespread feeling of outrage in the Sikh community. The country was paying a heavy price for the political mistakes of its leadership.

After the Blue Star attack when the temple was re-opened for visitors, anyone who went there came back to a huge crowd all anxious to hear about the situation. When the visitor would relate the tales of the ruined Akal Takht and bullet marks on the Golden Temple, Sikh women would weep inconsolably. The Sikhs have a proud history of sacrifice for the Golden Temple. When the raider Ahmed Shah Abdali had stopped the kirtans at the shrine and filled the holy lake with mud, Baba Deep Singh had led the Sikhs to free it. But Abdali was an outsider, an invader; when these beloved buildings were destroyed by their own country's army it became a more painful experience. The attack on the Golden Temple wounded the entire Sikh community deeply. Whether the government underestimated Sikh outrage when they planned the attack or whether they were unconcerned is still an open question. In 1988 during 'Operation Black Thunder' they had reached nearly the same situation, but things were handled better. Only two people were killed and the complex had been emptied beforehand. During Operation Blue Star the army, trained to fight foreign aggressors, thought of everyone in the Golden Temple premises as an 'enemy'. Even today, the price the country has paid after the attack and the massacre of 1984 cannot be ascertained.

Two

Not Riots but Murder

Surjeet Kaur's husband left the house to estimate the damage to the Nandnagri gurdwara when it was attacked on 1 November.

At the gurdwara a mob was waiting. Some of them dragged this unassuming trader in readymade garments along the rooftop and pushed him off. Others, below, beat him to death. After they had set fire to the gurdwara the mob turned towards Sikh homes in the vicinity, hammering at the doors. Inside, the women hid all the men in corners, almirahs and under the bed. The mob had only one demand, 'Get the Sardar'. Surjeet Kaur who had just lost her husband spoke out in tears, 'You have already killed the Sardar, where do we get him from now?' They went away for a while but came back in half an hour. Now they spoke politely, 'We have come to save you. Go to Punjab, no one will say anything.'

Surjeet's elder brother-in-law, hiding inside the almirah, asked again and again, 'Have the rioters left?' She would say, 'Nahin ji, not yet.' Remembering that terrible day, she says, 'We would give him something to eat and water from time to time in the almirah itself.' She still remembers his scared face as he hid in there.

Now the tone of the mob outside began to change. They said, 'Our mother has been killed, we will not leave you.' Surjeet replied that the prime minister was the whole country's mother. 'She was our mother too and because of this sadness even we have not eaten our dinner,' she told them. But they were adamant: 'Get the Sardar otherwise we will kill everyone.' The mob soon broke through the door and started burning down the house—some informer had told them that the men were hiding in the house. The beasts found each one of them before they could escape and threw them into the flames. They were still alive when they were thrown in.

The people in the mob were wearing dhotis and Surjeet Kaur had never seen them in this area before. Her younger sister-in-law's three-year-old son, Harpreet Singh Rikki, was also thrown into the fire but Surjeet Kaur managed to save him with some difficulty. These people attacked Rikki's father, first on the knees and when he fell, on the head. Then they doused him with the inflammable white powder and set him alight. They were doing the same with others too—it was almost as if they had been trained. Her son Tarwinder was somewhere—caught between the rioters and the fire. When she ran out to find him the mob pelted her with bricks. A brick hit her head and blood started pouring out. But she did not feel any pain. She felt as if her whole body had become numb, all that mattered was her son, she would think of the wound later. She found him hiding under a staircase, scared and injured, and managed to drag him back to the house. Tarwinder was then thirteen years old.

When all the men in the family were dead, the women saw that an elderly Sikh gentleman from their area, called Mamaji by all, was lying on the street, injured, but still alive. The mob had left him for dead. The women brought him home, but the mob came back—this time to loot. Despite his injuries, Mamaji got up and went to the door. He said that no one would harm the women as long as he was alive. The mob surrounded him and beat him to death.

Narrated to the author by Surjeet Kaur

The events following Indira Gandhi's assassination were not riots, though that is what they are commonly called. Riots break out between two factions in confrontation with each other and both suffer damage in greater or lesser degree. This violence was well organized. An estimated 5000 Sikhs died across the country, but there is no record of even one member of the mob being killed or charged. Violence began on the evening of 31 October, but on a minor scale. Sikhs were pulled off buses and motorcycles and beaten, and their pagris pulled off. The mobs at this point were not large.

Piecing together facts from affidavits and interviews given to the Nanavati Commission, a sequence of events can be arrived at. On the night of 31 October, a meeting of Congress leaders took place in Congress legislator Rampal Saroj's house where instructions were passed that the entire Sikh community had to be taught a lesson. To burn the Sikhs and their houses, sacks of an inflammable 'white powder' were procured from chemical factories and distributed all over Delhi. This powder is mentioned in many affidavits given by the survivors to the commissions of enquiry. No one had a name for the powder but they all said it was highly inflammable. Kerosene depots were told to make kerosene available. Sikh houses were identified and marked on the voters' list. The police was instructed to either turn a blind eye or to help the mobs.

A train was organized from Haryana to bring the mobs to Delhi. Similarly, Delhi Transport Corporation (DTC) buses were given the duty of bringing known criminal elements from Haryana—people with a record of killing and looting. The inhabitants of some Delhi slum clusters and illegal colonies which had been established as vote banks were roped in to join the mobs. When the Congress leaders had organized everything, the crowd was incited by provocative speeches to kill Sikhs. The mobs were assured that nothing would happen to them because the police, the administration and the government were with them. In fact the arrival of police spelt relief for the mobs, not the victims. As soon as there were any reports of Sikhs banding together for self-defence or to protect their gurdwaras, the police would reach the spot immediately in order to help the mob. If any Sikhs did manage to reach a police station, they were turned away. Some Sikhs who managed to call for help noted, in their affidavits to the Nanavati Commission, that they were told: 'Don't worry, we are coming to burn you too.' The logbook at the police station remained blank. Even the then police commissioner did not submit his logbook to the enquiry commission. Sikhs who had pulled out weapons to defend themselves were arrested. Such police behaviour was deemed bravery and several policemen were actually later given medals for bravery by the President, while Sikhs who used licensed arms to defend themselves were charged with murder and cases were filed against them.

The job of the police during the three days of violence that gripped Delhi was, one, to scatter Sikhs wherever they were collecting and two, to give the mob orders to attack, after seizing the Sikhs' weapons. As so many of the affidavits recorded by the commissions of enquiry set up to investigate the violence of 1984 have noted, this pattern was followed all over Delhi. First a crowd would gather and attack a gurdwara. If there was any resistance, the police would come to the help of the attackers.

The army was present in Delhi but it wasn't called out. The then army chief, General A.S. Vaidya told the Ranganath Mishra Commission that 5000 soldiers had arrived in Delhi from Meerut on the night of 31 October but they were not deployed. According to the affidavit of Tarlochan Singh, private secretary to President Zail Singh, the Lt Governor of Delhi, P.G. Gavai, told the President that bringing the army would disturb the situation further. When, three days later, the army was deployed, there was complete peace without a single shot being fired. It is hard to know why President Zail Singh could not prevent the massacre—many concerned citizens sought his intervention while the violence was raging in Delhi, but he was either unable or unwilling to take any action. The home minister Narasimha Rao's response was to ignore all that was happening. For three days the mobs were allowed to kill Sikhs and loot and burn their property. On the third day when the army carried out a flag march, all the disturbances stopped completely.

The pattern in which the violence occurred forced the Nanavati Commission to say, 'The massacre was organized and carried out with precision.' In the meantime malicious rumours were circulated claiming a train from Punjab had arrived full of murdered Hindus. This and other rumours served to dispel any sympathy the general Delhi public may have felt for Sikhs who were the victims of violence. In fact it was Sikhs who were being dragged out of trains and killed. Another rumour, very persistent and widespread, was that the Sikhs had poisoned the water supply of Delhi; another held that Hindus in Punjab were being killed. It is worth mentioning that Punjab is a state where there are nearly as many Hindus as Sikhs, but the two communities have never engaged in violence against each other. Even in the aftermath of the Delhi killings, there was no violence against the Hindus. The brotherhood between the two communities in Punjab cannot be found between any two communities in any other state.

The government television channel, Doordarshan—then the only televison channel—continuously broadcast scenes of Indira Gandhi's body kept in state at Teen Murti Bhawan and the slogan of 'blood for blood' that was being shouted by the crowds gathered outside. Avtar Singh Beer also mentioned this in his affidavit given to the Nanavati Commission. The channel emphasized again and again that she had been killed by her Sikh bodyguards, a departure from the convention that when reporting communal clashes, the term 'two communities' is commonly used to avoid inflaming passions any further. There was not even a single report on Doordarshan about the killing of Sikhs. The print media also failed to report on the massacres. Rahul Bedi, then a reporter with the *Indian Express*, broke the news of the Trilokpuri massacre after two days; other newspapers gave very sparse coverage. Looking at the media one could not have guessed that in the capital innocents were being mercilessly slaughtered. The media did not even deem it appropriate to talk to the widows of those killed. On 30 November, *India Today* put the local Congress leaders and police on the stand—one full month after the violence.

The massacre was not limited to Delhi: there was a loss of more than 200 lives in Kanpur and 200 in Bokaro, Bihar. In Patna, Daltonganj, Jamshedpur, Bhagalpur, Hazaribagh and Jhumri Talaiya, too, Sikhs were not spared. When the rumour spread in Lucknow that the Sikhs of Punjab had sent the Lucknow Mail filled with Hindu bodies, Sikh passengers were pulled out of trains at Lucknow railway station and murdered. The same pattern was repeated in Ghaziabad. Here, too, the Congress leaders operated in tandem with the police and this was repeated in Madhya Pradesh, Maharashtra and other parts of the country, areas where the Congress ruled. The Left Front prevented any violence from taking place in West Bengal and in

Maharashtra the Shiv Sena played a role in containing it. Khushwant Singh, writing in Dr Sangat Singh's book on the first 100 days of Rajiv Gandhi's rule, says that in Delhi itself more than 6000 Sikhs were killed. Indira Gandhi had been slain on 31 October; her funeral had been fixed for the afternoon of 3 November. The foreign press and representatives from all over the world were expected. The army carried out a flag march on the same day and everything quietened down.

In my view, the main accused in the Sikh massacre was H.K.L. Bhagat, and he became a cabinet minister in the Rajiv Gandhi government. Bhagat's constituency, East Delhi, was across the Yamuna. This was the area of the worst violence and had the highest numbers of deaths—estimated at between 1000 and 1500. Areas like Trilokpuri, Kalyanpuri, Jahangirpuri, Sultanpuri, were the worst affected. More than 500 Sikhs were killed in a single block of Trilokpuri—Block 32. Palam, Tughlakabad and Indrapur on the outskirts of Delhi were also among the worst hit—these were Sajjan Kumar's strongholds. Witnesses deposing before the Nanavati Commission recounted that he directed the mob from a police jeep. At that time he was a municipal councillor, but he was given a ticket to the Lok Sabha soon afterwards and became a parliamentarian. Dharam Dass Shastri, then an MP from Delhi, directed the killings in Patel Nagar and its adjoining areas, as witnesses have deposed before the Ranganath Mishra Commission. Jagdish Tytler has been accused of inciting the burning of the gurdwara in the Pulbangash area which led to two Sikhs being burnt alive. If anyone from the killing mobs was caught by the police, Tytler would turn up to release them, saying that they were Congress workers. Tytler was made a minister of state. On 19 November, Rajiv Gandhi, addressing a crowd at India Gate on his late mother's birthday, said, 'But, when a mighty tree falls, it is only natural that the earth around it does shake a little'; to the Sikhs it was like rubbing salt on their wounds. In the Parliament session after the massacre, not a single person referred to the tragedy that had befallen Delhi's Sikh community, though everyone condoled the death of former prime minister Indira Gandhi. The fact that the silence on the massacre cut across party lines is remarkable. It wasn't just members of the Congress Party that ignored the carnage on their doorstep. The Bharatiya Janata Party (BJP) leadership, including veteran parliamentarians Atal Bihari Vajpayee and L.K. Advani signally failed to raise the issue. There are reports that Sikh leaders approached Samajwadi Janata Party leader Chandrashekhar, who later became prime minister, to speak on the massacre in the

House. But he, while sympathetic, excused himself on the grounds that he did not wish to mar the mourning for Mrs Gandhi.

The Peoples' Union of Democratic Rights and the Peoples' Union for Civil Liberties published a report called *Who is to be Blamed?* giving details of the large-scale killings of the Sikhs and the role of the Congress and the police. But the courts did not take cognizance of this. In January 1985, Citizens for Democracy readied *Truth about Violence—A Report to the Nation* which also exposed the role of Congress leaders and the police, but the government did not take any action.

Meanwhile, the situation in Punjab started deteriorating and acts of terrorism increased and some Sikhs from pro-Khalistan groups went to Pakistan for weapons training. After the Sikh massacre in 1984, the sympathies of many in the Sikh community lay with them. No movement can gain ground if the sympathy of the people is not with them. Operation Blue Star and the Sikh massacre created the ground for this support. It was at this time that Prime Minister Rajiv Gandhi took steps aimed at resolving this situation and offered a compromise to Harchand Singh Longowal, the Akali leader. Before taking the compromise forward, Longowal asked first for an investigation into the massacre. This resulted in the setting up of the Justice

Ranganath Mishra Commission of Enquiry. Longowal was murdered in Punjab on 25 August 1985 and the centre has not acted on the Rajiv–Longowal accord to this day.

In the meantime it became apparent that the findings of the Ranganath Mishra Commission would prove to be a disappointment. It exonerated Congress leaders and did not result in any action being instituted against the culprits. Subsequently, investigation after investigation followed; some committees even recommended filing cases against the accused politicians but these were not acted upon either. Even the request that insurance companies be directed to compensate the economic damage incurred by the attacks on Sikh properties, was not accepted. The police started threatening those who had submitted their statements in front of the commission and there was a concerted effort to submit bogus statements in order to exonerate the guilty. In the end, when a few cases were registered, the witnesses were threatened and forced to change their statements, as the testimony of Sunder Singh Granthi to the Nanavati Commission bears out. Only a single First Information Report (FIR) was registered, that too in 1994. Everything was done to prevent justice from taking its course.

The Sikhs have moved on from 1984. The Congress has also had an attitudinal change which can be attributed to past lessons learnt and the influence of the Congress president Sonia Gandhi. Prime Minister Manmohan Singh has asked the Sikhs to forget the past. It is true that when somebody dies we advise their family with sympathy to put aside their grief and move on; but this happens if the death is natural. If somebody has been murdered it is hard to tell the bereaved to forget the murderers. If people have lost their lives in a natural cataclysm—an earthquake or a storm—it is a different matter; but how can a massacre be forgotten? Especially when there has been no justice. I emphasize that this is not a matter that should be politicized in any way; it should never become an issue to incite people towards violence in the name of old wounds. But forgetting is not a solution. One learns from history but does not forget it; indeed one should learn from history so that those mistakes are not repeated.

Jarnail Singh

The Attacks

Gurdwaras

It must have been the year 1995. I had then just finished my course in journalism and had begun freelancing for newspapers. During this time, on the martyrdom day of the ninth guru of the Sikhs, Guru Teg Bahadur, I went to Gurdwara Sheesh Ganj to pay my respects. This is the place where the Mughal emperor Aurangzeb had punished Guru Teg Bahadur for standing up against the forcible conversion of Hindus. Guru Teg Bahadur was beheaded on the emperor's orders because of this courageous stand. This example of the religious head of one religion giving up his life on the issue of the forcible religious conversion of another religious community is unique. It was this hallowed location that the mob attacked on 1 November 1984. It was the courage and the quick thinking of the police officer in charge, Maxwell Pereira, that stopped the attack on the Sheesh Ganj gurdwara. In the Kusum Lata Mittal Committee report there are descriptions of how the mob was about to reach the spot where Guru Teg Bahadur had attained martyrdom. They carried naked swords, iron rods and other weapons. But the Sikhs in Gurdwara Sheesh Ganj decided they would rather become martyrs than allow this sacred spot to be attacked. They assembled at Chandni Chowk in front of the gurdwara. The mob and the Sikhs were face to face, but Maxwell Pereira, the Deputy Commissioner of Police (DCP) of the area, felt that the situation was going to get out of hand. Unlike other police officers he did not ask the Sikhs to drop their arms but asked them to go inside the gurdwara, promising to protect it. The Sikhs went inside after his repeated requests, but as soon as they went in, the mob began pelting stones at the gurdwara. Because in other areas the police had been disarming and dispersing the Sikhs and then allowing the mob to attack them, the people who made up that mob assumed the same thing would happen here too. But in this case the police started pushing the mob back towards the Town Hall, where shops belonging to Sikhs were being burnt and looted. When Maxwell Pereira saw a Sikh-owned shop, Amrit Watch Company, set alight, he immediately ordered his men to fire on the mob. Perhaps this was the only such order given during those three days. Constable Shiv Parsan fired and a member of the mob was killed. To keep up the morale of those upholding law and order, Pereira immediately announced an award of Rs 200 for

Constable Shiv Parsan, indicating both to the police and the mob that breaking the law was unacceptable and would be punished. Kusum Lata Mittal in her report on the role of the police had strong praise for Pereira, noting that due to his timely action, the mob dispersed. Had this happened in the other incidents of mob violence against the Sikhs, the outcome would have been very different.

Gurdwara Rakab Ganj is equally sacred to the Sikhs and they have fought for it before. When New Delhi was under construction, the British had located the capital's important buildings—Parliament House, the Viceroy's House and the Central Secretariat—on Raisina Hill; they forcefully occupied the land of the gurdwara which was adjacent to these buildings. They even started breaking down one of its walls but the Sikhs held powerful demonstrations in protest and also courted arrest. This strong protest shook the British government and it backed down. On that day in 1984, however, a mob of some 3000 people converged on the gurdwara, surrounding it for nearly five hours. They attacked the gurdwara but could not go inside because the main door was very strong, but they brutally killed two Sikhs who had come outside the gurdwara. Witnesses have claimed in statements to the Nanavati Commission that senior Congress leader Kamal Nath was present and other witnesses have recorded statements that Delhi's police commissioner, Subhash Tandon, and additional police commissioner, Gautam Kaul, were also present. Subhash Tandon maintained in his own statement to the Nanavati Commission that he had not been informed by the officers under him of the violence that was rocking the city he was in charge of.

The mob that attacked this gurdwara had been paying their respects to the body of Indira Gandhi in Teen Murti Bhavan. A rumour started spreading that Hindus were being held captive in Gurdwara Rakab Ganj. The police searched the gurdwara and found that one of the sevadars was a Hindu, an employee of the gurdwara. Though he was brought out and it was clearly established he was alive and well, the attack did not stop.

Mukhtiar Singh, a sevadar, lived in quarters within the gurdwara's precincts. He recounted the sequence of events in his statement to the Nanavati Commission: at about eleven o'clock a large mob raising slogans against the Sikhs converged on the gurdwara. The attack lasted for nearly half an hour but the police, though present, did not take any action. The mob finally managed to break in but the workers and devotees somehow pushed them out. When an elderly Sikh bravely came out and requested them not to destroy this hallowed spot, he was caught and beaten and then set on fire. His son, unable to bear the sight, ran out to save him, heedless of the danger to his own life. The mob set fire to him too. The older man died but his son was still alive and the Sikhs inside the gurdwara somehow managed to pull him to safety. They begged the police to let them take him to a hospital, but the police refused to help. The boy succumbed to his injuries within two or three hours. Inside the gurdwara, a Sikh, Kanwarjeet Singh, had a licensed revolver. Looking at the crowd he fired a few times in the air. At once the police, which had taken no action against the mob, started firing in the direction of the gurdwara. They even went inside and arrested Kanwarjeet Singh. A case of murder was filed against him. Such police response was not an isolated incident; there were other cases where when the Sikhs tried to defend themselves, the police filed cases against them. In Kanwarjeet Singh's case, it was only after the matter of protecting the mob yet filing cases against the victims was condemned all over world that the government decided to withdraw the case against him.

According to Mukhtiar Singh, it was on the instructions of Congress leaders that several rounds were fired towards the gurdwara. Witnesses have noted that Station Incharge Hoshiar Singh gave his own service revolver to one of the people in the mob and asked him to shoot at the Sikhs. *Indian Express* reporter Sanjay Suri was present and reported the entire incident in the newspaper the next day. His statement to the Nanavati Commission notes that the whole crowd was being controlled by Kamal Nath though Kamal Nath's words to the crowd were not clear to Sanjay Suri. However Kamal Nath's presence in the midst of the crowd for two hours is established by Sanjay Suri's statement. Kamal Nath's presence has also been accepted by Police Commissioner (PC) Tandon. On the basis of this evidence, the Nanavati Commission asked Kamal Nath for an explanation for his presence. The commission in its report records that Kamal Nath could not provide a satisfactory answer as to what he was doing in the crowd for those two hours. The commission has also expressed its surprise at the fact that he was able to leave the venue without informing the police. The commission notes that in the absence of witness accounts, it is not possible for the commission to say that he was provoking the crowd to attack the gurdwara.

Trilokpuri

Trilokpuri, Block 32: 'In the morning I had watched my husband and ten members of my family hacked to death and now at night these bastards had come to take our honour,' says Bhagi Kaur. Ten people of her family had been burnt alive by the rioters, she recalled during an interview to this author. The memory still fills her with uncontrolled anguish and rage. The mob mercilessly stripped all women, still in a state of shock and disbelief at the death of their husbands and other family members in the morning. 'How many times we helpless, dependent ladies were raped by how many men, I can't remember. I had become unconscious. The drunk bastards kept on satisfying their sexual hunger. The men did not allow any of the women to wear clothes the whole night.' Saying this she breaks down.

Gopi, another woman from the locality, sitting near her, affirms this: 'Not even three dupattas are enough to wipe our tears,' she says. Nobody was spared—neither old women nor little girls. And there was no one they could call for as all the men in that colony had been burnt alive that morning—all 500 of them. When the women begged to be spared from molestation, their attackers asked them why they were being bashful since they no longer had husbands. 'If you try to run away,' their attackers told them, 'we will cut your breasts off.'

Bhagi Kaur had grown up listening to stories of how the Sikhs give up their lives to save women from dishonour. Of how they used to save Hindustan's daughters from being captured and taken into the military entourage of Ahmed

Shah Abdali to be sold in the markets of Kandahar. All their lives they had heard Hindu women tell them that if a Sikh was in a railway compartment or a bus, they would immediately feel safe. But none of this impeded the mob, who in the capital of this country abused these helpless, bereaved women the entire night. The organs of state and much of the media were mute about this outrage. It is only because the *Indian Express*'s Rahul Bedi managed to reach Block 32—despite police attempts to turn him back by telling him there was 'total peace'—that the news of the Trilokpuri massacre came out.

On the dawn of that terrible day, Bhagi Kaur says at that time that she had a television at home. After Indira Gandhi's death the broadcasts showed slogans like 'blood for blood' and 'kill the Sardars'. She was worried and asked her brother Indra Singh, 'Veerji, what is happening?' He said that whatever was written in their destiny would happen. However, he believed that nothing could. The whole block was inhabited by Sikhs and if 400 or 500 Sikhs got together, there was no way that anything could happen to them. But by then the crowd had started gathering outside the colony and stones were being pelted continuously. 'Then we came to know that three or four Sikhs near the colony had been killed. Everyone quickly decided to meet at Indra Singh's place,' recalls Bhagi Kaur.

The preparations to defend themselves against the attack had started. However, at this point, the police appeared on the scene—they not been visible since morning—so the Sikhs was felt safe; they thought the police would disperse the violent mob. Bhagi Kaur recalls that Station House Officer (SHO) Survir Singh Tyagi and Chowki Incharge Sharma came and started asking the assembled Sikhs to disperse and go home. 'We did not want to be separated but when the police offered to look after things we were persuaded. We placed our faith in the khaki uniform. This faith cost us so much. [Because of this] there is a whole colony of widows.'

As soon as the Sikhs went to their own homes the mob that had come from the nearby Chilla village attacked again. This time the police was with them. The mob broke off the pipes from the outer walls of houses, using these to smash windows and batter doors. They threw naked wires inside houses to frighten the inhabitants. Catching sight of a man called Bhai Samudra Singh they taunted him, saying, 'Come here, we will just cut your hair and then let you go.' Bhagi Kaur recalls 'The poor man said, "Sister if I die, please take care of my kids," ' and she breaks into sobs as she remembers this terrible moment. When the mob started beating Samudra Singh, his wife ran outside, trying to protect him by crouching over him. 'The brutes threw her off him and killed her husband.' Inside the house, Samudra Singh's brother, Sohan Singh, was crouched under the television, but he too was killed by a spear. His (Sohan Singh's) son-in-law Gurmukh Singh was hiding within some bedding. On the same bed was his one-year-old son, Hoshiar Singh. The mob killed Gurmukh Singh and set the house on fire, throwing Hoshiar Singh into the flames saying that he is the child of a snake and should be killed lest he bites us when he grows up. Bhagi Kaur managed to pull the child out with great difficulty.

The mob then dragged out Bhai Indra Singh and his son Manohar Singh. He was an 'Amritdhari' Sikh (a baptized Sikh). To really insult him they told him to cut his hair. He refused saying, 'I don't care if I lose my life but I won't quit being a Sikh.' The mob took him and his son to 'Peeli Kothi', a neighbouring house, and beat them to death.

H.K.L. Bhagat was supervising the mob, Bhagi Kaur says unequivocally. She remembers distinctly that he came wearing a kurta-pyjama and a cream shawl and said, 'No Sardar should escape', and 'The police will not say anything. Loot whatever there is to loot'. Also present in this crowd, says Bhagi Kaur, was Kishori Lal, known as 'the butcher' as he killed innumerable Sikhs with a butcher's knife. In the massacre of Sikhs, Kishori Lal is the only one of the killers to be sentenced to death by hanging for his crimes, but even in this case the court granted him life imprisonment. Amongst those present, according to witness statements, was Doctor Ashok alias 'Lambu' who played a leading role in the massacre. He later became a corporator on a Congress ticket.

Bhagi Kaur's two sons—Balwant Singh and Balbir Singh—were then aged two and five. Her daughters, Anita Kaur and Pinki Kaur, were then two years old and six months old respectively. Her husband, Lachhu Singh, had somehow survived death, hiding during the 1 November attacks on Sikh men and the molestation of women at night. The next day he took all the women and children and, moving quietly along the nallah, walked towards the Kalyanpuri police station.

But the mobs were on the watch for Sikhs; when they saw him, they beat him to death near the nallah itself. Bhagi Kaur had to leave her husband's dead body and together with other widows and children get to the Kalyanpuri police station. To their shock they saw a vehicle full of half-burnt bodies of Sikhs which had just arrived there. The stench was intolerable. In her statement she recalled that hundreds of bodies were piled one on top of the other in that single vehicle. Somehow from there they reached the relief camp that had been set up in Jhilmil Colony, and there endured eight months of impoverished and rejection-filled days. What was painful was the fact that relief material was pouring in for the victims from all over the world, but only a part reached these people. The Sikhs from the nearby Shahpur did help.

However, later in 1986, one of the policemen who had helped the killing mobs in the Trilokpuri massacre, Chowki Incharge Sharma, was posted as Station House Officer (SHO) in the rehabilitation colony of Tilak Vihar where the widows and orphans had been resettled. The victims of the riots were holding a religious function when he arrived. The widows recognized him—they had never forgotten. They surrounded him and started hitting him with their juttis. They tore off his uniform and threw away his cap. He was forced to run. Later the DCP came back with a large force—after all, his subordinate, the SHO, had been beaten publicly. He started throwing his weight about and asking the names of the women who had led the attack. Everybody said the same thing, 'Those who have lost their husbands have lost their identity.' He had to leave without taking any action.

A train of murderers

A train of murderers had come from Rohtak. At that time, about a hundred Sikhs from Nangloi had gathered at their local gurdwara and were defending themselves fiercely against the mob. Though outnumbered, the Sikhs held the mob off from the gurdwara. But on 1 November at twelve in the afternoon the scene changed completely. Confronted by hundreds of these killers who had come on the train armed with iron rods, sticks and other weapons and the inflammable white powder, the Sikhs were totally helpless. The organization behind this massacre is clearly revealed by the arrival of this train. The instigators were getting minute-by-minute information of where the Sikhs were putting up resistance. As soon as they came to know about the Sikhs defending themselves in Nangloi, this train was sent from Rohtak.

Gurbachan Kaur, in her statement to the Ranganath Mishra Commission, relates that after the death of Indira Gandhi when the news of attacks on the Sikhs began to spread, the Granthi Sahib of the Nangloi gurdwara announced on the loudspeaker that all the Sikhs in the vicinity should assemble at the gurdwara. Within a short span of time nearly all the men had collected there. Stones and bricks were pelted continuously but the Sikhs were holding out. This went on for about three to four hours. Then at about noon a train came from Rohtak and halted at the railway line nearby and a well-armed mob, numbering in the hundreds according to some reports, got off. The mob started setting fire to Sikh houses and to the gurdwara. Gurbachan Kaur hid in her Muslim neighbour Hamid's house. Her son Harbhajan stayed behind at the gurdwara itself. Now because of a mob of thousands and the fire within the gurdwara, the battle became difficult. Slowly, one by one the mob killed all the men in the gurdwara. Gurbachan Kaur's son Harbhajan was also killed.

Bishen Kaur also from the J.J. Colony in Nangloi, saw the train and the hundreds of killers who got off. She says that had the train not arrived, nobody from the gurdwara would have been killed. But because of the arrival of this train, the mob already present there was strengthened. Bishen Kaur's husband Kulwant Singh was killed in the gurdwara. Mahinder Kaur gave a detailed description of the killers to the Nanavati Commission. She says that they were like criminals and it was as if they were trained to kill people. They could kill a man with a single shot. It seemed as if they had killed people before.

This train from Rohtak implies that people from Haryana were involved. In her statement to the Ranganath

Mishra Commission, Gurbachan Kaur explains how they were defending themselves against the mob in the morning when they saw another mob of hundreds of people arrive in DTC and Haryana Roadways buses. Despite this the Sikhs kept on fighting them, but in the afternoon when nearly 2000 killers got off the train, the scene changed completely. They brutally beat their victims and set them on fire. Another victim Gurbachan Singh, who lost his father and his two brothers-in-law Amreek Singh and Trilochan Singh, said in his statement to the Nanavati Commission that he was taken to the police station and his long hair cut in the presence of Constable Rampal.

For Bhagi Kaur, the events of that fateful day have cast long shadows. She was allotted a forty-square-yard flat in the rehabilitation colony for the widows and orphans of the violence at Tilak Vihar. She had no savings—her husband used to be a porter and earned very little—but she had four children to bring up alone. All they had was burnt to ashes. The children did not study. The boys were traumatized by their experiences: Balwant Singh and Balbir Singh's joodas were undone by the mob and their long hair tied into braids; the mob also forced them to wear girls' clothes. The fear and humiliation had their impact on the boys. They boys fell into the drug habit. Balwant Singh is thirty-one years old today and is addicted to

Proxyvon tablets. Though he has a job at the Rakab Ganj gurdwara, he is always drunk. The second son, Balbir Singh, was set on fire, but saved in the nick of time by his mother. Balbir took to drugs when he grew up and later committed suicide. It might have been an overdose. Bhagi Kaur, who was working as a mali, came back one day and found the son she had saved from the fire, dead. Today, Bhagi Kaur asks, sobbing, 'Why was this written in my destiny?'

THREE

What the State Was Doing

The mob was chanting, 'Kill these Sardars, traitors of the country.' They first surrounded Mahan Singh and pulled off his pagri. As he bent to pick it up, they started to beat him, one by one at first and then together. His sons, thirteen-year-old Inderpal and eleven-year-old Harkirat, watched in horror from the roof. A few neighbours tried to stop the beating. 'He is an old army man,' they said. 'He has fought for the country.' Some people from the mob shouted back, 'How does it matter? Sardars are traitors.' The mob was hell bent on shedding blood. They hit Mahan Singh with an iron rod and he fell. Harkirat, unable to bear it, jumped off the roof to try and save his father. Seeing him, screams of 'We've got another Sardar' came from the mob. They fell on Harkirat and in the frenzy of their attack cut him into three pieces. Inderpal Singh was left watching his father and brother die. Even today, he starts to shake when he remembers the state of Harkirat's body. He says there were at least 500 people in that mob but not one face that he could recognize. He remembers that neighbours did beg for their family, 'Loot them if you have to, but don't kill them.' Their words had no effect. Had the neighbours found the courage to fight, perhaps things could have been different. Mahan Singh's widow, Baksheesh Kaur, now seventy-five, moved out of Trilokpuri where every

Sikh house had had a death in the family. She now lives in the widows' colony of Garhi near East of Kailash. Since 1984, when her husband and son were murdered, her family has never recovered. She has lost two sons to drugs. Today she just sits and weeps, still unable to understand the events that robbed her of everything she had.

Mahan Singh, a retired army havaldar, fought in the 1965 and 1971 wars against Pakistan

Helpless President, silent home minister

President Giani Zail Singh repeatedly asked his subordinates, 'Am I the President of a nation? Is there something under my control?' Evidence submitted to the Nanavati Commission records that when the President went to pay his respects to the slain Indira Gandhi at AIIMS on 31 October, his cavalcade was stoned by a crowd that had assembled outside the hospital. On the same day he had received a call from the Punjab and Sind Bank chairman, N.S. Basant. Basant's son-in-law, Kartar Singh Virdi, had been burnt alive by a mob in Patel Nagar.

Mrs Basant wanted to cremate her son-in-law's body and the situation in Delhi was so bad that she needed to approach the President of the country to ask for his help. But the President himself found it difficult to get an honourable cremation organized for Virdi. Having tried the home ministry repeatedly Zail Singh phoned the BJP leader Madan Lal Khurana for help. Khurana went to the Patel Nagar police station and met assistant police commissioner Ramamurti. Ramamurti said that it wouldn't be possible for him to hand over the body. When he was told that it was a presidential request, however, he said that the police could not give the body but what they could do was inform the family about the time and place of the cremation. They were told to 'come quietly'. The former chief justice of Punjab and Haryana, R.S. Narula, and Madan Lal Khurana have both verified this incident. Justice Narula even went to the extent of saying that the President was too apprehensive to come out of his residence.

The late Patwant Singh, the well-known journalist and architect, said in his affidavit to the Nanavati Commission that when he and a delegation of prominent Sikhs met Giani Zail Singh and asked him to stop the violence, the President's answer was, 'I have no right to intervene.' The delegation asked the President that when the nation was burning and innocent Sikhs were being killed and burnt on the streets, why he didn't have the right to stop this bloodbath, he didn't reply but stared blankly into space. When the Bangladesh war hero Lt General Jagjit Singh Aurora asked the President when the army would be called in, he was told, 'I am not in touch with Home Minister P.V. Narasimha Rao.' Lt General Aurora was stunned. Later, General Aurora was part of the Justice Narula Committee which investigated the riots of 1984. He also continued the fight against this injustice by constituting the Sikh Forum. His fight for justice was not appreciated by the central government; subsequently relations soured between the Bangladesh war hero and the government.

It is difficult to believe that the President of India could not get in touch with the home minister. The former chairman of the Minorities Commission, Tarlochan Singh, was then the personal secretary to Giani Zail Singh. He has said in his statement to the Nanavati Commission that when the President's cavalcade was attacked, the President had asked the Lt. Governor of Delhi P.G. Gavai on the phone, 'If the situation is so out of control then why isn't the army being brought in?' The answer was, 'If the army is called in, the situation is only going to get worse.' When BJP leader Vijay Kumar Malhotra spoke to the President, then too Zail Singh's answer was, 'I am helpless. I can't do anything.' This was also the reply he gave to Sharad Yadav, Karpuri Thakur and Chaudhary Charan Singh. His reply to each one of them was the same and is recorded in the affidavits to both the Ranganath Mishra and Nanavati Commisions. When the well-known journalist Kuldip Nayar met the President, he was told, 'Kuldip, neither am I being informed about the riots nor are any papers coming to me. If I am getting any information at all, it's through friends like you.' After this he became perturbed and said, 'I have no idea how the future generations are going to judge me.' Kuldip Nayar has recorded this in his statement to the Nanavati Commission. Former prime minister Inder Kumar Gujral also returned from the President's residence looking very crestfallen.

For a long time after the 1984 massacre, there was great resentment against Giani Zail Singh amongst the Sikhs. Ordinary Sikhs felt that when Indira Gandhi was killed, the President should have kept the reins of the country in his hands. What was the great hurry to make Rajiv Gandhi the prime minister? Kuldip Nayar has recorded that Giani Zail Singh later accepted that by doing so he had wanted to prove his loyalty to the Gandhi family. However, his relationship with Rajiv Gandhi steadily deteriorated from then on, so much so that many newspapers speculated that he even considered replacing Rajiv Gandhi. For the Sikh community, the fact that a Sikh was the President of the country and yet not able to save innocent Sikhs from slaughter is something they can never forget.

Home Minister Narasimha Rao was also inactive. When the well-known lawyer Ram Jethmalani went to meet him regarding the Sikh killings, he said little. In Jethmalani's account of the meeting to the Nanavati Commission, he reports that when he (Jethmalani) asked the home minister to do something to stop the killings, he got the answer, 'We shall see'. Narasimha Rao displayed a similar reaction when the Babri Masjid was being demolished. But such inaction was fatal for the Sikhs in 1984. The Ranganath Mishra Commission report says, 'If the army had been called in even by the morning of the 1st of November, at least the lives of 2000 innocent Sikhs would have been saved.' Though the commission is silent on who had the authority to do so, it is undeniable that the home ministry should have been the first to take a stand. Volume One of the Ranganath Mishra Commission reports states, 'One cannot believe the Police Commissioner's statement that he did not have a large enough police force.' In this regard the army chief General A. S. Vaidya's statement to the Ranganath Mishra Commission notes that by 31 October 1984 midnight, a brigade from Meerut had reached Delhi.

Later, the responsibility of the delay in the deployment of the army was placed on Lt Governor P.G. Gavai. But this was happening in Delhi, not in some remote and inaccessible part of the country. Why did it take two days to call in the army—two days during which Sikhs were being killed and their properties looted? The Nanavati Commission report puts the number of Sikhs killed in Delhi at 3000.

The police

After the assassination of Indira Gandhi, the situation was grave. The Sikhs in Sarai Rohilla were getting worried. They were told by the granthis from the gurdwara to assemble in the afternoon and be ready to defend themselves in case of an attack. In fact a mob attacked the gurdwara seven times, but each time a handful of Sikhs showed so much courage that the mob was beaten back. According to depositions before the Nanavati Commission, the police reached the scene after three o'clock in the afternoon and initially the Sikhs greeted their arrival with relief, thinking their long ordeal was coming to an end. The police asked all the Sikhs to go inside, saying that they would protect the gurdwara. The Sikhs were shocked to find that the police began to fire in the direction where they had asked them to collect. Five Sikhs were killed and many were injured. More than 340 Sikhs were killed in the Delhi cantonment area, but the police registered only five First Information Reports (FIRs) in which the names of the accused were not written. The language used in the FIR was, 'Rioters killed [number] Sikhs'. The FIRs did not record either the investigation or the name of the accused. Because of the way the FIRs were written, it was not possible for them to be presented in court.

Milkiat Singh, the secretary of the Shri Guru Sabha of Naraina Vihar, told the Nanavati Commission that when he had got in touch with the police regarding the killing of Sikhs, he was told, 'Whatever is happening is all right. Wait for a while, you will also be burnt.' Santokh Singh, a resident of the Maharani Bagh area, told the Nanavati Commission how the SHO of his locality came with two of his sub-inspectors and some constables and urged the assembled mobs through a loudspeaker to kill Sikhs and set fire to their property. Even when the police fired they did so in the direction where Sikhs were gathered together in their attempt to protect themselves.

Bhogal near Nizamuddin had a sizeable Sikh population. Here, according to Santokh Singh's statement, when the Sikhs tried to defend themselves the police dispersed them in different directions. Sixty-six trucks, five buses, seven cars, five scooters and ten motorcycles, Matador vans and jeeps were set fire to by the mobs under the protection of the police, a fact recorded in the Nanavati Commission report. Later, they could not even claim the insurance for these vehicles because the government also rejected their request that the insurance companies honour claims for property destroyed in the riots.

M.S. Sapra, a Sikh police officer, who was then SHO of Shahadra, dispersed the crowd gathering on 1 November in the Chajjupur area which was under his jurisdiction. Later, as he stated to the Nanavati Commission, when the mob started growing, he was asked by the assistant commissioner of police and deputy commissioner of police to go back to the police station because he was not acting in accordance with the rest of the police force. The 1984 Sikh Carnage Justice Forum has observed that Sapra was controlling the mob effectively, and was therefore insulted in front of the mob before being ordered to leave the scene by his superiors. Amarjeet Kaur who was present at the scene has testified to the Nanavati Commission that though she subsequently identified nine of those involved in the anti-Sikh violence in the area, not one of them was charged.

Sapra was not the only police officer who tried to do his duty and was stopped by his superiors. Ranbir

Singh, a resident of Karol Bagh, gave evidence to the Nanavati Commission on the incidents at the Karol Bagh police station which took place on 5 November. Here the SHO had started a campaign to recover property looted from Sikh premises and to arrest the culprits. The SHO managed to salvage property worth Rs 20 lakh from the mob and had even arrested twenty-four of the culprits. But Congress MP Dharam Dass Shastri and several metropolitan and municipal corporators including M.L. Bakolia arrived at the police station and demanded the release of the arrested people, threatening the police with dire consequences if this was not done. According to Ranbir Singh's statement to the Nanavati Commission, Additional Commissioner of Police (ACP) H.C. Jatav and Deputy Commissioner of Police (DCP) Amod Kanth were also present at the station. Even when Bakolia tried to beat up a constable right inside the police station, the constables refused to release the rioters; but H.C. Jatav advised the constables not to speak to national leaders in this way. These were not the only members of the mob that Jatav saved: when the police managed to catch six rioters in Indira Market in Karol Bagh, he had them released as well.

Barring a few exceptions, the Delhi police did little or nothing to maintain law and order. This is clearly exposed in the incidents at Samrat Enclave. On 1 November the police received information that a group of Sikhs had fired in self-defence at a mob that was threatening them. According to depositions made to the Nanavati Commission, the mob had had free rein of the area but the police had taken no action. As soon as the police heard about the firing they reached the spot where a house belonging to a Sikh was surrounded by a mob of over a thousand. As soon as the police arrived, they fired fifty-two rounds from their .303 rifles and nine rounds from their revolvers. The firing was directed not at the mob but towards the house. When the police entered the house, they found the bodies of three Sikhs who had died in the firing: two men and one woman. The house owner's terrified children were hiding in the barsati and were later taken to the Guru Nanak Public School relief camp by the police.

It was the same in other areas. Joginder Kaur, a resident of Sultanpuri's B Block, told the Nanavati Commission that the SHO, in the presence of Congress leader Sajjan Kumar, killed three Sikhs with his own revolver. In Nangloi where, unstopped by the police, the mob killed many Sikh families, Gurbachan Singh, a resident of the area, told the Nanavati Commission that he had somehow managed to reach the police station. When he asked to register a complaint, the SHO abused him and said, 'How come you bastards have escaped?' When his wife Gurcharan Kaur tried to register a complaint, she was thrown out of the station. In Chanakyapuri, the police received information that some Sikhs were hiding beneath the bridge behind the Akbar Hotel. The Nanavati Commission report has noted that when Station Incharge Mahipal Singh of the Chanakyapuri police station went there with a police force, he (Mahipal Singh) continued to fire in the direction of the bridge for a considerable period. When the police commissioner arrived, he, too, fired eight rounds. After a search they realized that no Sikhs were hiding there.

The police's pursuit of victims rather than perpetrators was amply clear in the shameful incident involving decorated air force hero, Group Captain Manmohan Singh Talwar, a resident of West Patel Nagar. On 1 November at around nine-thirty in the morning, a mob surrounded his bungalow. His garments shop was in the front portion of his house and the mob tried to break in. Talwar's neighbours came to his rescue and as the mob was small, it dispersed at this sign of opposition. But it returned two hours later and set fire to the shop, but the neighbours stepped in again and the mob went back. But around four o'clock that afternoon, the mob, now much greater in number—between 2000 and 3000 according to eyewitnesses—broke the door of the rear veranda and attacked the family. When one of them attacked Talwar with an iron rod, he realized his life was in jeopardy. He pulled out his licensed revolver and fired at the mob. In response the mob started throwing fire balls at the house—the barsati caught fire, but Talwar and his sons managed to douse the flames. The attack continued but the police did not turn up until around eight-thirty when they asked Talwar to surrender. By this time, Deputy Commissioner of Police Amod Kanth had arrived and he asked the group captain to drop his weapon. When Talwar refused, saying that he would only surrender to the army, they (the police) brought along an army major and Manmohan Singh Talwar surrendered. The bullets that he had fired to defend himself had killed five of the mob. The police took no action against the mob but booked him for murder. Amod Kanth was later decorated with a Presidential medal for his bravery.

Kusum Lata Mittal, a retired IAS officer, headed a committee set up to investigate the role of the police in the events of 1984. After completing the investigation, the committee declared SHO Soor Veer Singh Tyagi a 'living shame' to the name of the police for his role in the murder of 500 Sikhs in Trilokpuri. Tyagi managed to disperse the Sikhs who had assembled together to defend themselves; he then allowed the mob to attack them. He had threatened all the witnesses so that they were too intimidated to come forward. The Mittal Committee noted that through coercion, Tyagi got all the statements written in his favour and it did not seem likely the witnesses would have the courage to give a statement against him. Tyagi had taken out his own revolver and threatened Trilokpuri resident Santa Singh into surrendering his licensed revolver to the police. Subsequently Santa Singh and his son were taken into police custody, which allowed the mob to set fire to their house. Though 500 Sikhs were killed in Trilokpuri on 1 November, not a single person from the mob was arrested. Soor Veer Singh Tyagi was later promoted to additional police commissioner.

The Mittal Committee also noted that Tyagi's immediate superior, Deputy Superintendent of Police (DSP) Seva Dass, was an 'ugly blot' on the face of the police force. Dass had performed the task of removing Sikh police officers from duty so that the mob could have free rein and had told officers under him that there was no need to register any cases. After the 1984 violence Seva Dass was promoted to the rank of special commissioner.

The Mittal Committee noted that Delhi's Police Commissioner Subhash Tandon had refused to give his logbook to the committee. Tandon insisted his subordinates had not informed him of the violence taking place in the capital. Ultimately none of the recommendations of the many commissions and committees to take action against 145 police officers were acted upon; not a single case against any of the accused officials took its proper course. By the time the Nanavati Commission report was tabled, forty-two of the accused policemen had either retired or died. In just one case, the pension of a police officer was reduced.

The investigation carried out by Delhi's Police Commissioner Ved Marwah is an exception. Marwah started the investigation in November 1984 and seized the records of the violence perpetrated from all the police stations involved. The records indicate that during the time of the violence, concerned police officers vanished from the police stations. Complaints had started pouring in, but they were not registered and no action was taken. Ved Marwah observed that the main accused police officers had filed applications in the court to stop the enquiries, but the high court refused to comply. The accused police officers then started knocking on the doors of the government. As Ved Marwah has stated in the April 2009 issue of *Tehelka,* just as he had finished investigations and had only the job of writing the report left to do, he was asked to close the investigation. In the same *Tehelka* issue, Marwah stated that these orders had been given by the Delhi police commissioner, a post which comes under the home ministry. Subsequently, false cases were filed against Ved Marwah all around the country. Even subsequently, when he became the governor of Manipur and Jharkhand, he was still receiving summons for these false cases. Ved Marwah has put on record his disappointment that the police officers, who should have been punished for their role in the 1984 violence, were promoted instead. He openly questions the role of the politicians in this regard. Marwah has noted that when he became Delhi's police commissioner, he found that orders were in existence which specified that no Sikh police officer should be appointed to a high post. He managed to rescind these orders. In his interview to *Tehelka*, Marwah has stated quite categorically that there is no doubt that had the police used even a little force, violence on such a large scale could not have taken place in the capital of the country. The mobs would have dispersed. But this did not happen.

The Army

Captain Bereth of the Maratha Light Infantry of the Indian army just couldn't believe his ears. The mobs were going to burn houses belonging to Sikhs, but the district magistrate Brijendra Yadav refused to use force. Bereth, in his statement to the Ranganath Mishra Commission, recalled that Yadav said, 'Take your army anywhere you want, we will sort this out ourselves.' The mob set fire to the houses and two families including women and children, were burnt to death in the attack; in all about twenty-five Sikhs died. This horrific incident took place in Kanpur and subsequently the Ranganath Mishra Commission conducted an investigation against the main accused of the massacre, Brijendra Yadav. Yadav was not, however, punished for his role in the attacks.

In the eyewitness account that Captain Bereth has given to the Ranganath Mishra Commission he has said, 'It was the day of 1 November 1984 and round about 10 o'clock when my adjutant officer asked me to go to the police station where a joint control room for both the army and the police had been set up to take care of the situation. When I reached there I was asked by the officiating officer, Major P.N. Pandit, to go with the lady magistrate Tomar into the city and to follow her instructions in controlling the situation. I had an army unit and we went towards Kidwai Nagar. There itself we met the District [Magistrate] Brijendra [Yadav] who said that he would also accompany us. Between 11 and

11.30 we had reached Kidwai Nagar. Here I saw a huge crowd which was threatening to turn violent. Brijendra asked each one of us to get off our vehicles. My unit and I started taking our positions immediately. We left the main road and moved towards the ground where there were houses in the middle and the mob was surrounding them. When they saw the army, from somewhere people turned up and started begging us to save the people in the houses. I saw that the mob was at least a 5000-strong crowd.

'Now the District Officer came to me to try to get my opinion. He wanted to know whether we should go ahead and save the people in the houses or not. I told him very clearly that the crowd would have to be scattered. A curfew had already been imposed and if we followed it strictly, the crowd would go away. And even if it didn't scatter at least it will move 500 yards away from the houses. Then the army unit could go in the houses to save the residents. Actually, even I did not want to put in danger the lives of my men by sending them straight to the houses. Now the district officer left us and went directly to the mob and started talking to them. I don't know what he said but when he came back the police fired a few shots in the air. Even though nobody got hurt from these shots, the mob also did not move an inch from there. Before this, the district officer had had a chat with the mob.

'When the mob did not move, I asked permission to fill the form under IFD 908 for using army force in an abnormal situation. After listening to this, both the district officer and the lady magistrate refused to use the army and said that they don't want to sign. Then they turned to me and said that you leave, we will handle this ourselves. Soon after, the rioting mob killed members of two houses, looted their property and set their houses on fire.'

The Ranganath Mishra Commission noted the statement of Captain Bereth and asked a retired judge to investigate. What is important to note here is that despite a crowd of 5000 people, Yadav went ahead and spoke to them without any appearance of fear, a situation that led many to suspect that there was an understanding between Yadav and the crowd.

In Kanpur city, more than 200 Sikhs were killed, although according to the records of the government the figure is 127. Significantly, the army was already present in the cantonment area of Kanpur. According to Brigadier P.R. Kohli, at that time there were sixty-five officers, 159 junior commissioned officers and 2366 soldiers present. However, the army was not deployed, nor did the district magistrate allow Section 144 to be imposed. Even though there was a curfew in place, it was not strictly controlled by the police. The Ranganath Mishra Commission has expressed its surprise that given the fact that the army was present at the spot, it was not deployed on the night of 31 October. In Kolkata because of army deployment on that night, there was no massacre. Brigadier Kohli has stated that the army carried out a flag march and also a patrol, but they were not allowed to act against the mobs. The army cannot take action without the orders of the magistrate.

Deposing before the Ranganath Mishra Commission, Vinod Kumar Sondhi of Pandu Nagar reveals that he was at that time engineer at the IEC, a company in Panki, a suburb of Kanpur. When he was returning home from work he saw the house of his landlord, who was a Sikh, surrounded by a mob. The police as well as the city magistrate, Gupta, were also standing nearby. But they were doing nothing to either save the house or to disperse the mob. Additionally, Major Nayyar of the Maratha Regiment was standing nearby with his soldiers too but he, too, did not do anything. Sondhi went to the city magistrate and requested him to save the house. He got the answer, 'Be thankful that you are safe.' When he asked Major Nayyar to intervene, the major expressed his helplessness saying that he had orders only to stage a flag march, but none to take action against the rioters; in fact they could not even get out of their vehicles without orders from the civil administration. Sondhi, unable to think of anything else, ran towards the house and spoke to the mob: 'Police is here, police is here, run, they are about to shoot.' His statement had a magical effect: the mob disappeared. It is worth noting that if by merely shouting a few empty threats Sondhi could cause the mob to disappear, had the administration actually taken any steps at all, it could have saved hundreds of lives, as well as property.

This fateful inaction took the lives of Surjit Singh's family. Surjit Singh, a resident of Kanpur, stated clearly in his deposition before the Ranganath Mishra Commission, that district magistrate Brijendra Yadav was hand in glove with the mobs. His affidavit notes that Yadav spread the false rumour that Sikh soldiers in the cantonment area had shot and killed people in the nearby villages. This not only prevented the people of Kanpur from sympathizing with the Sikhs, it also served to incite the mobs. What is most surprising, however, is that despite Indira Gandhi's well-known connection with Allahabad and with Uttar Pradesh as a whole—she had been an MP from Uttar Pradesh for many years—the towns of Agra, Varanasi, Meerut and Bareilly did not experience violence of the magnitude witnessed in Kanpur.

I spoke to Awtar Singh of Damoli, near Ratanlal Nagar in Kanpur, who lost seven members of his family in the massacre. His father, Visakha Singh, his mother, Sawarna Kaur, brothers Jatinder Singh, Gurcharan Singh, Chatrepal Singh and Gurmukh Singh and his sister, Gurbachan Kaur, were first beaten senseless by the mob and then doused with kerosene and set alight. Reliving his memories he told me that he had no inkling that something like this was going to happen. 'On 31st night we all slept peacefully and the next morning [1 November] even got the milk and had breakfast. But then a mob descended from somewhere at eight in the morning. We decided to fight them thinking that we could stave them off till the police arrived. We didn't realize no one was coming to save us. The police themselves were a part of it.

'When these people saw that we were resisting them they began throwing fireballs into the house. The house was burning and there was smoke everywhere. We couldn't breathe. We thought that instead of choking to death, it was better to die fighting. My elder brother got out and tried to run away. He had run only a short distance when the mob caught up with him, beat him up right there with sticks, doused him with kerosene and then set him on fire. The same happened with a second brother afterwards. My parents died on the doorstep of the house.

Before that my father had given me the kirpan and asked me to run away. I had the kirpan in my hand, which is why the mob got a little scared and moved back a little and I ran to the police station.

'When I reached the police station, the police instead of helping me, snatched away my kirpan. They abused me and told me to get out. Now I had no option. I saw a dilapidated house nearby and I went there. I thought if the Lord wants I will survive. Fortunately, the mob did not come to know of this place and I escaped. But my family had been massacred. Later I even filed an FIR but the police did not investigate. Seven people had been killed from a single house but strangely there was neither a lawsuit nor any recording of statements. Of those killed, three brothers and one sister were married. I somehow took care of their families and children. But I cannot forget the injustice that happened with us. Those who advise us to forget should be treated like accused and punished for it.'

FOUR

The Men behind the Violence

Justice Dhingra asked her, had she, Darshan Kaur, seen him on television? To this, Darshan Kaur said, 'We don't have a TV at home so how could I have seen him?' The judge then asked, 'If he comes in front of you, will you be able to recognize him?' She replied, 'Yes sir, I will.'

'Take a look, is he around in the chamber?' She looked around but could not see him. She said, 'No sir, I can't see him.'

The judge asked her not to hurry, to take her time. Now, when she looked carefully, she saw he was hiding behind people who were all dressed in exactly the same clothes. She recognized him. Suddenly something happened to her and she pushed him with both hands. He fell to the ground . . . Darshan Kaur pulled off her chappal . . .

Seeing H.K.L. Bhagat, the whole scene floated before her eyes. She recalled how, dressed in a cream-coloured shawl, this killer had stood outside her house and roused the mob to attack. She remembered each word he spoke. Bhagat had said, 'Don't leave a single Sardar. They are traitors. Kerosene, weapons, all are there. The police is with you. Crush the Sardars.' Twelve men from her family had been killed at his bidding. In front of her eyes a tyre was tied around her husband's neck and set alight. The mob jeered, 'Look, a Sardar is doing the bhangra.' Her elder brother-in-law Gyan Singh's entrails had spilled out when his stomach was slashed. She felt as if he was still outside and the blood was still dripping from his body.

The accused prosper

H.K.L. Bhagat, one of the main accused in the 1984 massacre, was promoted from a minister of state to cabinet minister rank in Rajiv Gandhi's government. He stood in the Ashok Hall and took the oath to keep the integrity and security of the country intact. It was a sad day for many people, Darshan Kaur among them, but they did not cease their efforts to bring him to justice.

When Darshan Kaur pulled off her chappal when faced with H.K.L. Bhagat in Justice Dhingra's chambers, she was restrained by a woman police officer. The sight of him had brought back memories of the terrible massacre at Trilokpuri. On the night of 31 October a mob had set fire to the gurdwara, but the people living nearby had managed to put out the flames. On 1 November a much larger mob arrived. Congress leader Rampal Saroj was with them and quite soon there were cries of, 'Netaji is here, Netaji is here.' Bhagat got out of a car and could be heard urging the crowd to kill the Sikhs. Darshan Kaur recalled how after the men in the family were killed, she was raped, and her clothes burnt. Numb with grief and frantic with worry because her two-year-old son, Darshan Singh, could not be found, she shivered through the night, and somehow managed to walk to Patparganj to the Pandav Nagar gurdwara, hoping to find him. The smell of smoke filled her nostrils; the sight of bodies burnt so badly that it was impossible to identify them, swam before her eyes constantly.

The Pandav Nagar gurdwara proved to be an unsafe sanctuary and her son was not there (she did find him, but after three anxious days). That night—2 November—a mob attacked it. The people within managed to hold them at bay by hurling bricks and stones at them, Seeing Bhagat in the court brought it all back; she remembered all this and how she had had to watch her husband and his brother die. She told me, 'I was going towards him with a chair but the policewoman stopped me.' Still, she felt an overwhelming sense of relief that she had at least managed to threaten her family's killer with her chappal.

The journey to the court to identify Bhagat had been a long one. She had been going to court regularly and making her statements, when Atma Singh Lubana, who had been given the task of taking the women witnesses to the court by the Delhi Gurdwara Committee, turned up with Rs 50,000. It never occurred to the women to suspect he had been bought. The money was to persuade Satnami Bai, Darshan Kaur and Anwar Kaur to stop giving evidence against Bhagat. Darshan Kaur told me, 'When he [Lubana] came to me, he said that the money had been sent by the gurdwara committee. I kept the money. However, when my father came to know of this, he scolded me severely and said, "You are being sold and this is an advance from that." When I phoned Lubana he said, "Don't keep it with you, I will come and deposit it in the name of your children." Until then he had not asked me not to give evidence. But we found out when Satnami Bai turned hostile and refused to identify Bhagat in the crowd.

'When my date in court was coming up, Lubana came to my house the evening before. He brought a Sardar and two cut-Sardars with him. He kept 25 lakh rupees in front of me and said, "Take the money, your life will improve. Till when will you keep living like this? Two of your sons are unemployed and one is trying to make a living by driving a three-wheeler. How long will you live like this? Keep this money and we will buy you a house in Rajouri Garden as well." I said, "Tell me if you can bring back even one person from those twelve people?"'

When Lubana and his companions saw her in this frame of mind they ran away and she called 100 to contact the police. She was then taken to the Raghubir Nagar police station where some paperwork was done and she was told to go home. Some time later when she was coming out of the court one day, three men on motorcycles brandished a gun at her. She escaped by hiding inside a nearby shop. After this, some twenty people attacked her near the gurdwara—Atma Singh Lubana was among them. Darshan Kaur was hit on her nose and forehead and she started bleeding from the blows. She was in the hospital for ten days, but the harassment did not stop.

When another court hearing approached, she thought she would eat at the langar at the Mata Sundari gurdwara of the Delhi Sikh Gurdwara Organization Committee first. Here, after asking committee member Mahinder Singh Matharu to organize for a vehicle for her to go to and from the court, she went to eat at the langar. Just then Atma Singh Lubana, who was also a member of the committee, turned up. He started abusing her. He said, 'You can still do what I say and refuse to be a witness.' But the other people at the langar, hearing his words, caught hold of him, some even threatened him with their chappals. He was handed over to the police. A case was registered and he did not get bail for three months. Subsequently, the court pronounced a three-month sentence which was taken as his punishment period. Later he had to go to the Akal Takht to ask for forgiveness. Not only this, he had to ask for forgiveness from the riot victims and the community association.

But in the end, the Nanavati Commission decided not to prosecute Bhagat because he was by then in pitiful health. He died soon after.

The Nanavati Commission report recorded the statement of Moti Singh of Sultanpuri which said, 'Sajjan Kumar declared to the mob that had gathered that whoever has killed Roshan Singh and Bhag Singh will be given a reward of Rs 5000. Whoever will kill the other Sikhs will be paid Rs 1000 per person. At this, Congress leader Chuttbhauja Nathu Pradhan came forward saying he would take this work to a logical conclusion.' Police records show that more than 400 Sikhs were killed in Sultanpuri itself. Moti Singh lost two of his grandsons. One policeman who was trying to save the Sikhs was asked by his colleagues why he was wasting their 500 rupees.

The maximum number of Sikh casualties was recorded in the trans-Yamuna area which was H.K.L. Bhagat's area.

Sajjan Kumar's stronghold was Outer Delhi which included areas like Nangloi, Palam etc. On 14 October 1987, the Jain–Banerjee Committee, set up on the recommendation of the Ranganath Mishra Commission, asked the police to register a case of murder based on the statement of the riot victim Anek Kaur. In her statement in 1985 Anek Kaur described how Sajjan Kumar and other Congress leaders had incited the mob to kill Sikhs. Sajjan Kumar and his relative, Jaikishan, who later became an MLA himself, had come together in a jeep. Jaikishan had said that only 'six Sardars are left, let's kill them quickly too'. Sajjan Kumar had replied, 'Hit them so much that none of them survive.' Anek Kaur's husband, Vakil Singh, was killed there.

Subsequently, Anek Kaur, having deposed against Sajjan Kumar in 1985, succumbed to pressure. She changed her statement in 1994 and said that she had not seen Sajjan Kumar. How long could a poor, lonely widow take the pressure? Misri Kaur, Anek Kaur's sister-in-law, has said that Anek Kaur was told that all her expenses would be paid for life, and a flat would be given to her as well. She was paid for a while but that stopped after two years.

The Jain–Banerjee Committee made many recommendations, but nobody listened. Even the media discovered two months afterwards that the committee had recommended that a case be registered against Sajjan

Kumar. When the matter came to light, a stay order was taken. The matter remained pending in the court for two years. Later, when the CBI began its investigations in 1990, this matter was allowed to hang for another two years. The CBI did not even submit the challan.

By this time the Narasimha Rao government was in power at the centre; he had been union home minister during the 1984 carnage. Narasimha Rao did all he could to hide the whole investigation and matters related to it. He did not give the CBI the permission till 1994 to submit even the accusation letter in the court. Only when Jagmeet Singh Barar, a Congress MP from Punjab, raised the matter in the Lok Sabha, was there was some movement.

During this time, BJP leader Madan Lal Khurana became chief minister of Delhi and promised to get justice for the Sikhs. When the Jain–Agarwal Committee, set up in 1990 during the tenure of the V.P. Singh government, recommended that cases be registered against Sajjan Kumar, H.K.L. Bhagat, Jagdish Tytler and Dharam Dass Shastri, the Lt Governor of Delhi, Markandey Singh, agreed. The central government tried its level best to remove Markandey Singh from his post in order to ensure no action was taken on the twenty-one statements which formed the basis on which the cases against the political leaders had been registered. When the Delhi government approached the CBI it was told that they were overloaded with work and could not, therefore, look into these matters. The CBI, till date, has the same attitude. Subsequently, when Delhi chief minister Madan Lal Khurana, asked the Narasimha Rao government for an affidavit against the accused, the government did not provide one. When Khurana threatened to go to the Human Rights Commission, the affidavits were given. But the Delhi pclice were not under Khurana's jurisdiction: if the police decided not to register a case, there was nothing the chief minister could do.

Later two weak cases were registered against Sajjan Kumar, but inevitably, they did not stand up in court. One was dismissed on the grounds that after twelve years the statements of the witnesses did not match fully; in the second, the FIR did not even have Sajjan Kumar's name.

When the Nanavati Commission called Sajjan Kumar, he said that the statements against him had changed, but had no answer when Justice Nanavati asked him why there were accusations against him. Justice Nanavati wrote in his report that since Sajjan Kumar and Congress party worker Balwant Khokhar, who was charged with being the main conspirator, killer and leader of the mob, were influential people in their area, their acquittal from criminal proceedings could not be given much importance, therefore fresh cases should be registered against them. After this, on the recommendation of the Nanavati Commission, three cases were registered against them in August 2005. In one case, Nirpreet Kaur (*see Chapter 6*) recorded a statement against Sajjan Kumar and in another, six witnesses testified to having seen Sajjan Kumar. Despite this, the CBI has still not submitted accusation letters in the two cases.

Sajjan Kumar was acquitted in 2002, by which time an ailing Anek Kaur had died. The judge, however, expressed his unhappiness at the outcome, saying, 'The CBI has fully failed in proving matters against the accused.' What is surprising is that the CBI took five years to challenge this judgement of the court. In March 2007 the CBI submitted the names of three more witnesses who had seen Sajjan Kumar lead the mob. The CBI itself says that Jagdish Kaur, wife of Jagsher Singh, gave a statement that she had seen Sajjan Kumar inciting the mob in the Delhi cantonment area. In her statement to the Nanavati Commission Jagdish Kaur said that when she was going to the police station on 2 November, near Mongolpuri, she heard Sajjan Kumar tell the gathering, 'No bloody Sikh should survive.' When she reached the police station she overheard the SHO say, 'How many chickens have been roasted?' The police had earlier not registered her statements and for the past two years the hearings have been pending. The question is that when the CBI had witnesses, why did it take them five years to challenge the lower courts? The FIR had been filed twelve years ago and another two years have passed since their submission of names.

After the Nanavati Commission report in 2005, the CBI took action by recording the statements of witnesses. Jasbir Singh, from Rajnagar, says that being a Congress worker he knew Sajjan Kumar, and his associates Balwant Khokhar and Mahinder Singh Yadav by sight. But when he reached the police station to file a report he was told to register a report for destruction of property, and that there was no need to report the names of any people. He still took Sajjan Kumar's name but the police did not register a report. Similarly, Surinder Singh of Ludhiana made a statement to the Nanavati Commission that he saw Sajjan Kumar at the scene of the killings; Kher Singh, another witness, has given a similar statement. There are witnesses, but justice is still to take its course.

After Indira Gandhi's murder, the Pulbangash gurdwara, in the West Delhi stronghold of Jagdish Tytler, was attacked. After burning down the gurdwara, the irate mob killed retired inspector Thakur Singh and his helper Badal Singh, who were inside. The main granthi of the gurdwara, Surinder Singh, survived. From his position on the roof, he saw the whole scene. In his affidavit to the Nanavati Commission he said that on 1 November, the mob under the leadership of Jagdish Tytler had attacked this gurdwara near Azad Market. Within a week of the massacre, Tytler went to Surinder Singh with two blank papers in his hand and asked him to sign. But Surinder Singh refused.

Surinder Singh in his statement to the Nanavati Commission spoke about Tytler's leadership of the mob. But when Justice Nanavati questioned Tytler, his immediate response was that Surinder Singh Granthi had given a subsequent statement in which he denied the first statement on the grounds that he did not understand English and therefore he hadn't known what was written in it. Justice Nanavati expressed his surprise at Surinder Singh's second statement and questioned Tytler on how he had come to know about the second statement. The Nanavati Commission report recorded the commission's view that the second statement had been given under some pressure. It noted that if the witness had not seen Tytler in the crowd, why did his first statement declare that he had? And why did he wait till 7 August 2002 to make the second statement which was a total reversal of the first? When the Nanavati Commission submitted its report it said that there was concrete evidence against Tytler and the matter should be registered.

Ten days after giving his second statement, Surinder Singh went to Canada. He was a worker of the Sikh Gurdwara Organization Committee, but he went on leave without collecting his dues, leading to speculation about the source of his funds. Later when he came back to India, the gurdwara committee sent a notice to him asking him about his second statement. He replied on 23 March 2004, 'If you want my reply give me the guarantee that the committee will be responsible for my life and any destruction of my property.' The committee did not send him any further notices, but two months later, the then president of the committee, Prahlad Singh Chandok, a former Congressman, was seen garlanding Tytler and presenting him with a kirpan at a function. The matter reached the Akal Takht through the Sikh Forum, a body set up by General Aurora, but despite this, no action was taken. When the whole Sikh Sangat criticized Surinder Singh Granthi, he gave another statement in front of the CBI on 12 February 2008 which reiterated his first statement against Tytler. He said that the second statement had been under duress from Tytler. In an interview to *Tehelka* in 2008, Surinder Singh said, 'If I get killed, Jagdish Tytler will be responsible for it. Tytler put pressure on me and took my signatures on blank papers. I was threatened that if I went against him my family and I would be killed.'

The second witness against Tytler is Jasbir Singh who saw Tytler lead a mob near Kingsway Camp. He lives in the United States and initially the CBI said that they did not have his address. Even after he told the media that he was in America, the CBI did not get in touch with him. When the court ordered that his statement be recorded, a few officers were sent there to take it. Later the CBI called him an unreliable witness and asked for the matter to be closed. The question is, can the CBI decide that a witness is unreliable? If such a decision has to be made, surely it is the responsibility of the court?

An article in the *Indian Express* of 25 April 2009 by Ritu Sareen noted that in an internal report, the joint director and the deputy inspector general of the CBI admitted the case against Tytler in the riots of Bara Hindu Rao had substance. But despite this, the then CBI director Ashwini Kumar decided to give Tytler a clean chit. The CBI rarely closes high-profile cases, but it told the court that it did not want to continue its investigations. When the *Indian Express* spoke to Jasbir Singh, he said that he was surprised that the CBI had called him unreliable when he had told them that he had heard Tytler's words to the mob outside the Guru Teg Bahadur Hospital. According to him, Tytler said, 'When nothing is going to happen [to you] after killing the Sikhs then why have you killed only so few of them?'

Jasbir Singh said that when the CBI officials had come to take his statement in America they told him that this case was going to go nowhere. Jasbir Singh said that he had told the CBI earlier that two other witnesses, Roshan Singh and Chain Singh, people from the same locality, who now lived in Canada, had also witnessed Tytler's actions, and were ready to give their statements on this matter. But the CBI did not speak to them.

Ever since he has lost his Congress Party ticket after I threw the shoe at Chidambaram's press conference, Tytler has still not answered these questions: if he is not responsible for any killings then what has he done to get justice for the people who were killed and the victims who where robbed in his area? As a high-ranking political leader of the area, he could have thrown his weight behind the move to get justice for the victims of his area. Why have many witnesses said they were pressurized to make statements in his favour? When the police arrested some people from the mob, why did he go to the police station to rescue them? If he says that he has fifteen FIRs in which he has the proof that people from the Rashtriya Swayamsevak Sangh (RSS) were involved in the violence, why has he been silent for the past twenty-five years? Why doesn't he expose them and fight for justice?

After the shoe-throwing incident when he was denied a Congress ticket he accused me of being connected to the Akali Dal and said that the incident was an Akali conspiracy. I want to make it clear I am not connected to any political group and I have refused all offers to join politics or to support a particular party. I only protested against an injustice that has continued for twenty-five years.

After she was attacked by Lubana, the court has given Darshan Kaur extra security. Now there are guards outside her house. Wherever she goes, a PCO follows her. Darshan Kaur is bitter about the fact that Sikh leaders did not take care of the widows who suffered so much. Had they provided some support, these poor, vulnerable widows would have been witnesses and the accused would not have gone scot-free. Her eyes fill with sadness—for her it is another blot on this terrible chapter in the history of the

Sikhs. Does she feel justice has been done? No, she says, even if Bhagat is dead, Tytler and Sajjan Kumar are alive, and she now takes the CBI to people who witnessed the two men giving the mob orders to kill Sikhs. She claims that she has introduced the CBI to eleven such people.

When I went to meet Darshan Kaur at her residence, she had bought a garland to honour me. But I placed the garland around her neck. She had retained her courage unflinchingly—succumbing to neither bribes nor threats. She was the one who deserved it.

FIVE

The Aftermath

Baljeet Kaur from Tilak Vihar, who has been looking after her four daughters and a son since she was thirty-five years old, does not want to say anything bad about her husband Raju Singh who died of the drug habit. 'When he is no longer alive what is the point in talking about the times when he used to beat me or take drugs?' He was an auto driver but would spend all his earnings on drugs. If Baljeet Kaur tried to stop him, he would turn her and the children out of the house. They complained at the police station, even put him in the drug de-addiction centre for one and a half years, but it was to no avail. Now the futures of seventeen year old Paramjeet, sixteen-year-old Gurpreet, twelve-year-old Jassi, ten-year-old Pinki and nine-year-old Fateh Singh is worrying her so much that it is affecting her health. Her father-in-law, Sawan Singh, was killed by the mob in Trilokpuri, so how does her household run? When asked this Baljeet's voice constricts with tears. She says, 'I get flour sometimes from the Fateh Nagar gurdwara and sometimes from the Rakabganj gurdwara to feed my children.' She ekes out a living by washing utensils and doing housework in people's houses.

Narrated to the author by Baljeet Kaur

Jarnail Singh

Orphans of a massacre

Until Satpal was thirteen, she was the life and soul of her family. Her laughter would echo through the house all day. She was just moving from childhood to adolescence and her joie de vivre was still unselfconscious and infectious; she didn't have a care in the world. But she changed overnight; she had to. Her parents and brother were murdered before her eyes and between one hour and the next she went from carefree child to surrogate mother. She had three little sisters—the oldest of whom, Balvinder Kaur, was ten, Mahinder Kaur was eight and the youngest, Surinder Kaur, was just two. Satpal was then in class eight but after that day in November 1984 she never went to school again. It's been twenty-five years since Satpal's life changed irrevocably, but to her it feels as if it happened only yesterday.

The family lived in Nandnagri, in Delhi's trans-Yamuna area. They were comfortably off, certainly enough for their father, Sahib Singh, to spoil his daughters shamelessly and give them whatever they asked for. In time-honoured fashion, their mother, Nishan Kaur, would tell him not to pamper them so much—they would get married and would have to adjust to life in their *sasural*, but he never listened. 'Why shouldn't they have fun now?' he said, always adding, 'Besides, we will get our daughters married in well-to-do families.'

On that fatal November day the four sisters were playing as usual when their mother came and gave them a good scolding. 'She was looking very disturbed,' Satpal recalls today. 'I knew something was wrong. She often got worked up but she never ever said a word to us girls. In fact, she'd say, "You go play. This is your age to play."' However, that day she looked more than worried, but nobody had the courage to ask her why. Her husband had gone to his lathe work factory in Anand Parbat, but had come back early.

He was talking to their mother in hushed tones, clearly worried about something. The Sikh neighbour who had just come in also wore a troubled look. The only words she heard were, 'Indira is dead, it is better if you stay put at home.' Satpal and her sisters couldn't understand why if somebody as distant as the prime minister had died, should *they* be worried. 'Nobody from our house has said anything to anyone,' she remembers thinking. 'Our elder brother is here. Even he doesn't pick fights with anyone.'

The day passed with this sense of unease, even fear. Every now and then they heard shouts and other noises coming from outside, but they were not alarming enough to really scare the little girls, yet their parents and brother were clearly extremely tense. 'After all, this is Delhi, the capital of India, not a far-flung village that people can do anything,' Satpal remembers her father saying, but she sensed he was not reassured by his own words. Next day when she woke, she saw her father's eyes were red from lack of sleep. He started getting ready for work, but when her mother told him not to go, he agreed without protest. As the day progressed, the cries outside grew louder. They were calls of 'blood for blood' which Satpal heard without really understanding. But fear had begun to grip her; her heart was racing.

It was towards evening when the neighbours—a family that ran a hairdressers' shop—came to their house. These neighbours told Satpal's family not to be scared, to remain indoors. They said they would lock the front door of the house from outside, so that people would think there was no one home. 'We couldn't understand anything, but thought that because of the situation turning dangerous, they were being good neighbours and were doing what good neighbours should do,' Satpal says. 'We thought that they had come like gods to save us. If the door was locked from outside, the mob would assume no one was at home and turn back. How intelligent our neighbours are, we thought. After all we should help each other.'

But soon after, the same neighbours arrived with a

huge mob. 'Now we understood that they had locked us up to prevent anyone from escaping.' Her father quickly locked the door from the inside. Until now she had watched people die only on screen, on films and television serials, with rivers of ketchup flowing. But this was real. Death was at the doorstep. Suddenly the mob armed with weapons, kerosene and an inflammable white powder set fire to the motorcycle outside. Satpal's father had given the bike to her brother and no one around had such a bike. After having burnt the bike they started throwing burning tyres and the inflammable white powder inside the house. Satpal's family didn't know what to do; they had no idea. Where could they get help; who could they ask? The police station was right in front of the house, but despite the fact that such a big and noisy mob had gathered, there was no sound of sirens. Were they asleep? Had they run away out of fear? These were the questions in Satpal's mind as they waited inside the locked house with the mob's cries growing louder and louder outside. 'Father addressed all of us sisters and our brother Devinder who was seventeen years old then. "Children, now we can only be saved if the police arrive. Otherwise we shall all die." My brother did not waste any time. Jumping from the back and somehow leaping over the walls of the neighbouring houses, hiding in the lanes and bylanes, he managed to make his way unnoticed to the police station opposite to beg for help.'

Satpal had now climbed on to the roof. She was relieved to see that her brother had reached the police station—now the police would come and they would be saved. She saw him begging the policemen to save his family. But then her heart turned to stone. The lawkeepers were telling him, 'Go away from here!' They were kicking him, screaming at him. 'Will you get the police station torched also?' But her desperate brother did not want to leave the police station empty-handed; they were his family's only hope. When he did not stop begging and pleading, they turned their guns towards him. Now there was nothing for him to do but to run. 'I think that had he simply run away from there, he would have survived. He was outside the house and had he hid in the lanes, he could have escaped alive. But as soon as he stepped out of the police station, the police wasted no time in showing their true colours. They began to fire at the very person who had asked them for help.' One such bullet hit her brother in the back and went right through his chest. He fell and did not get up.

The police did not want a witness who would reveal that they had refused to help. Or perhaps they wanted their bit of credit for having killed a Sardar. Satpal didn't know.

She was on the roof watching her brother die, shocked beyond belief. She had been screaming but she could not bear to go down and tell her parents that their son had been so brutally murdered. She stood there shell-shocked, then made her way downstairs. Her parents, who had heard the bullets, saw her tear-stained face and realized that something had gone terribly wrong. Meanwhile the mob, baying for the blood of Sardars, had started throwing the burning tyres inside the house. Realizing that the police were on their side had emboldened them.

Most people in that crowd were from the poorer areas just outside Nandnagri. During elections, the Congress had used them as a vote bank, giving them money and liquor; today they had been given complete freedom to loot the Sikhs. People from this basti had often asked Satpal's father for jobs in his factory. Today she recalls bitterly, 'People who had asked us for work were determined to destroy us.' Despite this, her father did not give up. His elder brother, who had retired from the army, was inside the house; together they decided to go out and face the mob, now a thousand-strong. It was just as if a pair of deer had decided to fight a pride of lions. But they also had no choice; they had to try something. They shut the children inside a room and began to defend themselves—throwing bricks, stones, whatever they could lay their hands on at the mob. But they couldn't hold them off for long. The mob had broken the door and surged inside. The three adults were murdered right in front of the children's eyes. They were first hit with iron rods till they were nearly unconscious; then they were tied up, doused with the white powder and set fire to. Satpal began to go into shock. The mob would not let them cry—when they cried, they were threatened with the same fate. Seeing her mother, father and uncle die in front of her eyes, Satpal lost consciousness. She felt she was dead too. When she came to, she realized that she had survived; she couldn't give up. She crept out stealthily from the still burning house. All around was the stench of burning human flesh.

There was a pattern to the mob attacks. They targeted Sikh men; few women and girls were killed. But because Satpal's mother tried to stop them from killing her husband, they killed her too. Girls were not touched. Eight-year-old Mahinder clutched Satpal's dupatta while Satpal carried her youngest sister Surinder in her arms. Surinder was crying from hunger—she hadn't had any milk since morning. How could a two-year-old know that she had lost the protective presence of her parents? Suddenly, Satpal discovered Balvinder was missing. Had she, too, been massacred by the mob? Satpal was frantic.

When all the Sikh widows and children were taken by the army to the relief camp of the Bangla Sahib gurdwara, she too managed to go there. After the incident the girls found their Sikh neighbours in the camp who were also victims of the violence. They took in the children—managing to find some milk to feed Surinder. The whole day the relief camp reverberated with the desperate cries of people, still in shock over the experiences they had undergone. Devastated women wept uncontrollably as they were reunited with their families, who broke down themselves when they saw the condition their daughters, daughters-in-law and sisters were in. Those who had lost loved ones to painful, horrifying deaths were inconsolable. Satpal had been in the camp for eight days when she heard Balvinder's voice. She had found Balvinder. The sisters clung together; it was as if they had been apart for eight years and not eight days. For the first time they allowed themselves to grieve for their parents and brother. Balvinder refused to let go of her sisters for even a minute. The two younger girls would wake up night after night saying, 'They are killing Mummy and Papa', and Satpal, herself still a child, would have to comfort them.

When nobody came forward to claim the girls, the three were sent to Nari Niketan (a home for destitute women). Their maternal grandfather in Alwar had been frantically searching for them. He could not have come any earlier as the situation in Delhi had been so bad. When this old man, broken by the death of his son-in-law, daughter and grandson reached the home, the girls clung to him. They remembered their visits to him in their summer vacations—finally here was a familiar, secure presence. Thankfully, they left the home and went back with him to Alwar. Their grandmother was ailing, so it was hard for her at her age to take on the responsibility of four children. Satpal decided to quit school and stay home and help her grandmother take care of her younger sisters. The younger girls went back to school.

In the face of the public outrage at the massacre of Sikhs, in 1986 the union government allotted flats in Jehangirpuri, on the eastern outskirts of Delhi, to the victims. The flats were like pigeonholes, tiny and cramped, but Satpal came here with her sisters because if she had not somebody would have acquired this house illegally. Since the girls were far too young to live alone, their grandfather decided to move in with them—their grandmother had passed away before. He used to get a small pension and the gurdwara gave some Rs 400 to all victims of the violence—but this was not enough to live on. Satpal, now fifteen years old, decided that she would not say no to any work, no matter how back breaking.

She stitched clothes, making pieces for the dyeing machine and even worked as a maid. She worked day and night, rarely earning more than Rs 200. The money was just enough for their humble living but fell horribly short when someone fell ill or there was an unexpected expenditure. Satpal's sisters would borrow old, used books; they wore old clothes and ate very simply. There were no treats; no extravagances that other children enjoyed routinely. Satpal was both their mother and their father: from giving them baths, dressing them, feeding and putting them to bed—just keeping them alive despite all odds—was her responsibility. This, along with the back-breaking work she did to support the household.

After some time, they came to know that the high court had ordered that all victims of the anti-Sikh violence were to receive Rs 1 lakh each as compensation. Once this was announced, relatives who had till then refused to help, came forward to take custody of the girls. Fortunately, the judge decided that the girls would receive the money only after they turned eighteen. And so it happened, when Satpal turned eighteen she withdrew the money and her grandfather got her married. Now the question was—where would the younger sisters go? Who would look after them? Satpal had looked after them since she was thirteen; she couldn't just leave them and walk away.

Her husband, who was an autorickshaw driver, was kind and supportive; so she was able to take them with her to her new home. Satpal started a new life with her sisters, but it wasn't easy. It was a small house and she was just married, but she had to look after her sisters too, who were living with her. When Balvinder turned eighteen she withdrew the money from the court and was married off; so was Mahinder. Satpal and her grandfather couldn't think of any other solution. Only the youngest, Surinder, who had been just two at the time of her parents' death, did her MA and is now an assistant to a doctor. The girls have survived, but at tremendous cost. Remembering how she brought up her younger sisters brings tears to Satpal's eyes. She says, 'We were like princesses but this massacre turned us into beggars.'

Despite losing everything Satpal did not lose courage. She fought to bring those neighbours who had turned traitors to justice. How could she forget those who had destroyed her life? But this wasn't easy. The accused thought that they could put pressure on the young girls. They put tremendous pressure and the girls were threatened practically every day. They were told, 'We will do the same thing to you that we did to your parents and brother.' When the girls didn't pay any heed, they attempted to bribe them. When this too did not work they began sending the women from their houses to cajole the children. Satpal was fed up and when she started receiving threats right inside the courtroom, she suddenly told the judge one day, 'Sir, these people are threatening and forcing me to change my statement.' When the judge put the people threatening her behind bars, Satpal felt emboldened. Previously she had felt intimidated by the atmosphere in the courts. Now Satpal would go on every date. The accused got punished but their punishment was a mild one.

The house had to be sold at a pittance but they were so short of cash and she was too scared to go back to living in that house. Dealers had a field day and gave her very little money. This happened with all the Sikhs whose houses were burnt and their widows and children were too scared to return home. What is amazing is that Satpal didn't even come to know how many times her factory got sold on its own, that too without proper documentation! It was when she started asking about it that she found out that it had been sold several times. When she asked the neighbours there to help her, they refused to recognize her and said, 'Girl, we don't even know you.'

The factory might be worth crores today but Satpal does not have the strength to fight the court battle. Who knows how long the case will go on? The lawyer would also have to be paid. She says now she doesn't keep well. She has two sons and a daughter. If they complete their studies, she will be content. 'I feel as if in these thirty-seven years I have lived several lives.'

'When will peace be found?'

Shanti Kaur was filled with foreboding. Her 22-year-old son Sohan Singh had not come home. There were just twenty-three days left for his wedding on 30 April 2009. Did he not like his prospective bride in Rajasthan? He had looked happy about it but he hadn't called and none of his friends knew where he was. After two days of worry, she went to the police. They washed their hands off the problem, saying, 'Must be somewhere with his friends.' Shanti Kaur had seen her father Kirpal Singh and brother Modu Singh being burnt alive at the hands of a mob in 1984. Later, her husband died of throat cancer. She had no father, brother or husband. Would she lose her son as well? She wondered if she should tell the girl's side, but decided it would be too insulting. She decided to wait for a few days.

Shanti Kaur had pulled her son Sohan Singh out of the quagmire of drugs after a lot of effort. But the drug traders had killed him for refusing to buy any more. His body was hidden in his house, beneath the bedding. The murderer, Kamal, was so arrogant, that he did not even try to get rid of the body, confident no one would go to the police. People say Kamal had murdered his own brother too. When the body started to smell, the house-maid noticed. The news spread, but the body couldn't be identified as its face had been mutilated. Hearing the news, Shanti Kaur went to the house. She recognized his clothes and his chappals. The long shadows of 1984 had destroyed everything she had.

The police were not ready to register a case of murder. But when the people from the colony surrounded the police station, they rounded up the killers. Shanti Kaur took a loan for the funeral and said prayers for her son and grieved not just for the boy whose future had once momentarily seemed brighter, but for all the others she had lost as well. She was living in Block 32 of Trilokpuri with her father Kirpal Singh and brother Modu Singh when the mob burnt 500 men alive as the police stood by. At that time Shanti Kaur was seventeen but she could not understand why the mob was bent on killing them. In front of her eyes her father Kirpal Singh and brother Modu Singh were tied to a charpoy. First their long hair was cut off and then they were set alight as casually as the burning of Ravana's effigy on Dussehra day. Even today Shanti Kaur hears the cries of her burning father and brother. She had just turned eighteen when relatives married her off to Puran Singh. Puran Singh's father had been hacked to death by the mob in Sultanpuri. Even Puran Singh had been slashed with swords and knives and left for dead. He used to earn a living by selling vegetables, but it seemed then that her life was coming togther again. During this period they had three children—Sohan Singh, Rajni and Gurbachan Singh. However Puran Singh's health was deteriorating. He was becoming weaker day by day and he talked of pain in the neck where he had been slashed by a knife. They did not have enough money for treatment at a good hospital though Shanti Kaur suggested a number of times that he should see a doctor at a good hospital. At this he would say, 'When we have a bit more money then we shall see.' But that day never came.

When he was diagnosed with throat cancer they found that the treatment would cost lakhs. Where could they have got so much money from? Shanti Kaur was helpless. He expired within a month in front of their eyes.

Shanti Kaur did not give up and started working in homes to bring up her children. Since she was not educated her options were very limited. When she started going to work, people engaged in the drug trade pushed

Sohan Singh towards the drug habit. He would remain sad and tired all the time. When Shanti Kaur would ask, 'Son, what has happened?' he wouldn't reply. When she probed his friends, their reply shocked her. Sohan was addicted to smack. When he couldn't get it he would become frantic, thrashing about as if he was going to die. His breathing would slow down, his throat would dry up and his legs would hurt so much that he could not stand. Shanti did not know what to do. The fifteen-year-old son would understand his mother's pain and ask her to poison and kill him. But how could she do that? Then he would cry for her to save him. She took him to the gurdwara many times and made him swear that he would not take drugs but when he would have the craving, he would forget everything else.

Neighbours suggested that she should send him to a de-addiction centre where he could be treated: he went repeatedly to centres at Aman Vihar, Rohini, Paharganj, and Govindpuri. She tried everything to get her son treated. For some time he would lose the habit but later he would again fall in with the same company and the addiction would start again. In the end he was admitted to the Nihal Vihar Centre. He was kept there for nearly one and a half years and she paid for the expenses by working in homes. Shanti Kaur's smile began to return when her son left drugs completely. After he returned home he stayed away from drugs and the company of the drug addicts. When he started working she was relieved. She felt as if her sacrifices were bringing results. When I was listening to her tell her story, I could not imagine a sadness greater than this. Shanti Kaur's daughter Rajni is sixteen years old now. When she started going to houses to work, the people around started saying all sorts of things. The younger son has left his studies and works in a clothing shop but she is worried about her daughter's marriage. She asks, 'When will peace be found in my life?'

This is not an uncommon story. Far too many of the children of the victims of 1984 are addicted to drugs. After the death of their fathers, their mothers were compelled to go out to work and there was no one to take care of the kids.

Gopi Kaur said bitterly in an interview to this author that the accused in the cases of violence deliberately got the children of the widows' colony addicted to drugs so that their whole generation would be destroyed and there would be no one left to raise a voice about 1984. This is the position held by Jagdish Singh, president of the Sikh Riot Victims' Action Committee, and all the widows are of the same view. But the despair of the widows is understandable. After losing seven people including her husband in the massacre, Gopi Kaur's hopes were centred on her son, Gurmeet Singh. But when he was twenty-two years old, Gurmeet fell into the drug habit, became addicted to smack, and died of his addiction. Her younger brother-in-law, Chandu Singh, is so emotionally scarred from his experiences in 1984, he can't go out of the house. He is so scared of the sight of a khaki uniform that he starts running when he sees a police officer. He just sits, staring blankly in front of him all day. Gopi is one of the seventy unfortunate women who received compensation as victims of 1984, but unscrupulous people robbed her of even that. A bogus company called the Oriental Housing Society came into being and lured the uneducated, vulnerable widows into depositing their money into this scheme, promising higher returns. In six months this organization vanished. The widows curse them till today and a case of fraud is being fought in the courts. However, there is little hope of getting the money back.

Two of Barfi Kaur's nephews lost their lives in the prime of their youth by taking drugs. The terrible events of 1984 cast their long shadow, blighting even the lives of young people, who grew up in an atmosphere of the despair and bitterness of their families who had lost everything. Many of the widows feel the people responsible for their husbands' deaths are also to blame for all that has befallen them since. The same people have blocked the course of justice and continue to protect the perpetrators.

Barfi Kaur and the other widows who got together in Jagdish Singh's house to talk to me said that in the widows' colony, more than 200 young men have lost their lives to drugs. She recalls that when she and the other widows of the colony used to go out for work, which they were compelled to do as their husbands, the family wage earners, had been killed, kids in the age group of ten to fifteen years were targeted and lured into the drug habit by unscrupulous pushers who preyed on unsupervised young boys. There are few households in the colony where the scourge of these intoxicants is not felt. The desperation among the addicts is such that they will even take drugs meant for animals to satisfy their cravings. Young children sniff whitener after pouring it on a handkerchief. Sniffing petrol and other substances is quite common. They can finish a whole strip of Proxyvon-1 tablets in a day. There are frequent thefts to pay for the habit. They sell anything, from the neighbour's motor pumps to household clothes and utensils. If families refuse them money, the atmosphere in the house degenerates into abuses and fights.

The widows' hopes were centred on their children. They hoped their sons would do well, but for many households in the widows' colony, this hope too has dwindled. A tearful Gopi says, 'I lost seven men from my house in the riots but now I cannot tolerate the pain of losing my young son.' The head of the Sikh Riot Victims' Action Committee, Jagdish Singh alleges that there is a well thought-out conspiracy behind the spread of drug addiction in the widows' colony perpetrated by those powers that are against the riot victims. He says, 'If this was not true then at least the police would have been with us. We have requested help from the SHO, SP, DCP, but not one is prepared to listen. The drugs are being sold openly in the form of medicines and injections but there is no one to stop them. They are tired of complaining but the police does not take any action. Proxyvon and other drugs are freely available at chemist shops but there is no stopping them. Why is it so?' The situation is such that the day Jagdish Singh complained about the drug business to the police, his house was burgled the same night. Perhaps it was a warning.

Jagdish Singh says that ever since the riot-hit families have recovered a bit and started asking for justice, the drug dealers have one by one started giving away the drugs free of cost. Whether this is a conspiracy or not is difficult to say, but as the people in the area ask constantly, why aren't the police taking any action?

Baljeet Kaur has looked after her five children—four daughters and a son—since she was thirty-five years old. Her husband Raju Singh died of the drug habit. Her father-in-law, Sawan Singh, was killed by the mob in Trilokpuri but her husband, too, was in a way a victim of the same violence. The black aftermath has left its mark on many lives. Asha Kaur's husband Arjun Singh, too, used to take drugs with other addicts at their haunt in Block B, next to the cemetery.

Maya Kaur fails to understand God's larger plans. In 1984 her father Bhoja Singh was murdered by the mobs. Later, when she married Dilip Singh, poverty forced her to come back to live with her mother Himmat Kaur in the latter's flat in Tilak Vihar. She became a mother to five kids and lost her husband to drug addiction. He wasn't an addict before coming here, she says, but the question that obsesses her is how to bring up five children, a question that stares the mother–daughter duo in the face, both having lost their husbands.

After her husband's death, Devi Kaur's elder brother-in-law turned her out of the house. She is back home after a lot of problems. But Lakshmi Kaur's predicament is the worst of the lot. When as the mother of four girls and a boy, Lakshmi Kaur lost her husband, Joginder Singh, to drugs, the rest of her family turned her out within twenty-three days of his death. Now she is forced to live in a rented accommodation. Twenty-one-year-old Ranjeet Kaur has a three-year-old daughter but she started having fights with her husband Satnam Singh over his drug habit and now they are divorced. This young woman is now facing the prospect of an empty life ahead but does not know what to do. She is somehow surviving by doing sundry jobs in houses. Tearfully she says, 'We are daughters of Sikh families but I have to work as a maid outside and we have to even throw stubs of bidis and cigarettes in the dustbin. When will our own people [Sikhs] think about us? If anyone complains to the police they beat up these youngsters and send them back instead of trying to stop the drug trade.' More than 200 youths have lost their lives to drugs and who knows how many more will fall into this quagmire. It is not easy for these people to get them admitted to drug de-addiction centres. At these de-addiction centres it costs Rs 2500 per month which they can ill afford. To cure the youth of their drug habit Devendra Jyoti of a non-government organization, Asra, wants to work with them using behavioural therapy but he is not getting any space for this.

The fallout of the violence of 1984 is still destroying the families of the victims.

From Venky to Tihar

The date was 18 October 1988. Tihar jail was full of activity. Nirpreet Kaur was lying down in the special cell. Suddenly she heard a motherly voice, 'Baby, are you asleep?' Nirpreet got up with a start. She was hearing this voice after several years. In front of her was her mother Sampurna Kaur who had also been locked up in this jail under the charge of giving shelter to terrorists. Mother and daughter wept as they clung to each other. Nirpreet's ten-month-old son began to cry too. She told her son not to cry. She told him she was his nani (maternal grandmother). This was the first time that the grandmother was seeing her grandson. The mother had been locked up on the charge of sheltering terrorists and the daughter had been brought from Punjab to Delhi just a day before.

Nirpreet had been caught under Operation Black Thunder. Post-Operation Blue Star many hot-headed youths became activists after seeing the 1984 Sikh massacre. They wanted to take revenge. Once again they set up posts inside the Golden Temple complex. To flush them out, Operation Black Thunder had been carried out in 1988. A student of the second year graduate programme, speaking fluent English, studying at the famous Delhi college, Venkateshwara, in 1984, Nirpreet had never imagined that she would one day meet her mother like this in Tihar. But watching her father die at the hands of the mob in the 1984 Sikh massacre, she lost her bearings. She could not forget how he had been immolated again and again.

Before 31 October 1984 she was living happily in Rajnagar in Palam with her father Nirmal Singh, mother Sampurna Kaur and brothers Nirpal Singh and Nirmolak Singh. Nirpreet still remembers that the day former prime minister Indira Gandhi was murdered her father had come home at four o'clock. Out of breath he told them that the taxi stand which was owned by Sikhs next to the Moti Bagh gurdwara had been set on fire by a mob. Somehow he had managed to save his taxis and now he would go and check them the next morning. Balwant Khokhar who was the nephew of the then councillor Sajjan Kumar and owner of an oil depot came to their house in the evening. He came to her father and said, 'Sardarji, allow my brother to join the taxi service.' Nirmal Singh responded to this untimely request by saying that if any car was free he would let him know. Then her father started to talk about the bad situation. Nirpreet who was standing there with the tea tray heard Balwant Khokhar say, 'Sardarji, don't worry. My mama [maternal uncle] is a councillor here, don't go anywhere, we will not let anything happen to you.'

She says today, 'We understood later that he had actually come to find out the exact number of people in the house. Rajnagar had 250–300 Sikh families and Nirpreet's entire lane belonged to Sikhs.

Nirmal Singh's usual routine was to get up at one-thirty and take the Lord's name and do his daily oblations. On 1 November 1984 too Nirmal Singh got up at the same time. After oblations, he went to the gurdwara and started the kirtan for 'Asaji di var'. Suddenly, he noticed that there was a policeman standing outside. When the officer was questioned, he said that the situation was bad therefore he was there for protection. When more people started joining in the prayers the officer vanished. Everybody felt that something was wrong. Nirmal Singh had just got home when the mob attacked the gurdwara. Perhaps the policeman had come to survey the place before the attack. Nirmal Singh was worried that the mob would insult the Guru Granth Sahib. On her father's instructions, Nirpreet and her younger brother quickly entered the gurdwara from the back. They both carried the Guru Granth Sahib on their heads and ran towards their house. But the mob had spotted them. The crowd ran to attack them. Her brother Nirpal received a few blows but he escaped. Then their father came out and asked the local crowd why they were hitting children. The Sikhs were getting together.

Balwant Khokhar and Mahinder Yadav, the owner of a bakery, pushed the crowd but the mob while leaving set fire to a truck belonging to one of the residents of the lane, Harbans Singh. Instead of getting involved with the mob, the Sikhs doused the fire. But they had seen bestiality in the eyes of the mob—the atmosphere was charged with it. It was decided that since the situation was bad they would all get together. For this Nirpreet's house was selected. It was the one in the corner and could be defended from all four sides. Since most of the Sikh families were owners of taxis and trucks, they had access to bottles of petrol.

On 2 November morning, the crowd attacked again. This time the crowd had come armed with more weapons and inflammable oils and chemicals. But the Sikhs were also prepared. They showed such courage that they had the upper hand with the mob. The Sikhs had twelve–thirteen kirpans. The women and children also started throwing stones at the mob. Nirpreet says, 'We knew that it was impossible to leave from there. We had to fight for as long as possible.' When the Sikhs showed their courage, Balwant Khokhar and Mahinder Yadav fell at her father's feet and said, 'All of us are brothers, this bloodshed is not okay.' By then the police had arrived. Khokhar and the police officers said, 'Let us reconcile. Come with us.' The other Sikhs told her father, 'Don't go.' But Nirmal Singh said that the police are with us and if this situation can be resolved, it should be. He felt that now that the police were present, he would ask that the damage done to the gurdwara be repaired as a part of the resolution.

How could he have known that this was a trick. The mob felt that the Sikh defence started from the house of Nirmal Singh and killing him would end the Sikh resistance. Khokhar immediately handed over her father to the mob and said, 'Here, take the Sardar you had left behind. I've brought him.' Nirpreet was in the crowd and because she was a woman nobody noticed her. They set her father on fire. He was burning, but still managed to stand up again. At this, Nirpreet remembers, Inspector Kaushik, who was standing there, said to the mob, 'Die in shame Gujjars—you can't even burn one Sardar.'

Nirpreet continued her story: 'Then a man who we used to call Ishwar Sharabi [drunkard] got kerosene to pour over my father. When he was set on fire, he jumped into a nallah nearby. Father's dastar had opened. He was pulled out and tied with ropes. Now the wife of a man called Dua who was from the nearby 'mohalla' (colony) also got a can of kerosene. When I tried to stop her she said that the Sikhs deserved it. Father was immolated again—badly burnt this time, but he still managed to jump into the nallah again. The crowd felt that he was dead, but despite being badly burnt, he was alive. When they saw him breathing, the priest from the Shiva temple said, 'Arey, kill him otherwise he will not spare you later.' Then Mahinder Yadav threw white powder on Father and Balwant Khokhar hit him with a stick. This time when they immolated him, Father could not get up.' Nirpreet's eyes blaze when she says this. With the police by their side, the mob killed quite a number of Sikhs.

It was actually a Sikh neighbour who was in the air force who called for an air force car to rescue the beleaguered men and women. Nirpreet related, 'I used to tie the dastar those days myself but before we sat in the car my hair was braided. So they couldn't make out that I was a Sikh.' After this, Nirpreet never tied the dastar again.

Then they were in an air force officers house in Palam. The night was spent without sleep and early morning the sound of kirtan was heard. Nirpreet's mother recognized the voice and said, 'Child, it looks as if it is your father's acquaintance Rawail Singh doing kirtan.' When they asked around they came to know that the sound was coming from a gurdwara at the Palam air force station a few kilometres away. At that time everything was wild like a jungle there. When they reached the gurdwara they met Sardar Rawail Singh and Wing Commander L.S. Punnu.

They knew that looting was taking place but had no knowledge that Sikhs were being killed. Doordarshan and the newspapers were reporting no such news.

The air force people gave them their car to go and see the condition of their house. Nirpreet recalls that on the way she saw Sajjan Kumar in a police jeep telling people, 'Not a single Sikh should remain alive. If anybody tries to save them, burn their houses too.'

When she reached her house, their Hindu neighbour, Soni, saw them. He said, 'My child, I wanted to save your father.' At that time an angry Nirpreet told him, 'I have seen everything with my own eyes. I know what you were doing—you were with the mob and never stopped them from killing Father.' She believes it is possible that Soni then went to Balwant Khokhar and told him that Nirmal Singh's daughter was still alive, had witnessed everything and was now at the Palam gurdwara.

While this was happening, someone had left milk and biscuits for the Sikhs who had taken refuge in the gurdwara. But the way they had been left created suspicion in the minds of the Sikhs. These suspicions proved correct; later, when the milk and biscuits were tested, they were found to be poisoned. Wing Commander Punnu pulled out his gun and tried to follow the person who had left them, but he had vanished. Two months after this incident

Wing Commander Punnu was crushed by a truck near the Palam air force station while he was out on a morning walk. Nirpreet has no doubt that this was murder and not an accident.

Nirpreet, along with her family, had now started living with other victims of the 1984 violence in the Moti Bagh gurdwara camp. But she constantly felt under threat. In the end she decided to go to Punjab and she took admission there in the Lailpur Khalsa College. The atmosphere in Punjab was then highly charged. Here she came in contact with the All India Sikh Students' Federation and in 1986 married Gurdev Singh alias Roshan Lal Bairagi who was wanted by the police in a number of terrorism-related cases. Nirpreet returned to Delhi and started living in hiding, but Bairagi was arrested. Till today the police lists him as an absconder but according to Nirpreet he has been killed in an encounter. The police wanted to catch Nirpreet too, but well-wishers advised her to go into hiding in time. She escaped to Punjab. The police arrested her mother, Sampurna Kaur, and a neighbour, Lajwanti Kaur, and took them away. They were framed for giving shelter to terrorists. Her mother was locked up for three years. During this time the mother–daughter duo managed to meet each other occasionally. And this was also the time when Nirpreet reconnected with the

Federation in Punjab and was arrested under Operation Black Thunder on 15 May 1988. By this time she had a ten-month-old son. When she was brought to Delhi she saw her mother again.

She says at first the senior officers had refused to let them meet, but a sympathetic warden called Anita, who was in charge of the prisoners, allowed it. Hearing her mother's voice after a long time was a great solace for Nirpreet and the grandmother saw her grandson for the first time. Nirpreet had been locked up under the notorious Terrorist and Disruptive Activites (Prevention) Act (TADA). However, when her mother's bail application was granted by the judge, the lawyer R.S. Sondhi informed the judge that her daughter and grandson were also in the lock-up and made a request for their release on bail too. The judge passed the order for Nirpreet's bail. However, some cases against her were still pending in Punjab, therefore she was taken there. Once she got bail, she placed her son in the Badu Sahib Academy near Solan.

During the 1991 Lok Sabha elections, a few incidents of firing on some accused Congress leaders took place in Delhi. The police took Nirpreet into custody for an enquiry. She had been returning after meeting her son in the Academy when the Chandigarh police caught her. The police could not prove anything, so the court eventually acquitted her of all charges in 1994.

Relatives asked her to start her life afresh and in 1997 she got married again. But perhaps happiness was not in her destiny. The person she married had been married before and she was his second wife. He died some years later. Nirpreet has a son from him too.

Despite being acquitted of all charges, the police still bother her though for the past one year she has been free of their visits. Does Nirpreet regret the path of life she chose? She admits, 'Yes, I had never thought I would go this way. Now I want the accused [in the 1984 violence] to be punished by law.' Nirpreet says today, 'I paid heavily for it but why are those who killed my father still roaming free? Is this justice?' adding that she was compelled by circumstances and now her activism entails helping other victims other victims to fight their cases. She says that she has been fighting the case for four riot victims because these victims don't have the money to pay for a lawyer. She is involved in bolstering the confidence of those witnesses who are scared of giving statements. She says that she has convinced the wife of Badal Singh who was killed in the Pulbangash gurdwara to come and give a statement (the court has agreed to include Badal Singh's wife Lakhwinder Kaur amongst the witnesses in this case), and is also helping the CBI in their investigations.

Has she ever shared her life story with her son? She says, 'He knows. When I was locked up in jail there was talk at home about my release. He would tell his grandmother to get me out. At that time she [the grandmother] told him that they would need a lot of money to get me out. Coincidentally, right at that time money was being collected to buy my brother a truck and he saw that. He created a racket saying you are not getting my mother out but buying a truck for Uncle.' But Nirpreet confesses she is pained when her son questions why he was born in a Sikh household. Today the boy has cleared class twelve but always says that he wants to leave the country and settle abroad.

SIX

Why I Hurled the Shoe

My questions were different and so close to my heart that I started getting emotional. Perhaps all the pain from a long time had come together today. Chidambaram's reply was technically politically correct. The case was sub judice. And the judgement was pending. But sometimes in sensitive matters, technical replies do not work. Chidambaram had just expressed his happiness over the clean chit that had been given to Tytler. He was talking about the matters being in court but I wanted to hear something more. Perhaps I had expected a more sensitive answer from Chidambaram. But his attention today was focused on how the Congress election manifesto dealt with terrorism, and the Bharatiya Janata Party and Lal Krishen Advani were the main targets. I asked if Tytler's case was not being dealt with as part of a strategy. When the hearts of the victims have been bleeding for a long time, how can anybody be happy? Will the Sikhs not get justice? Instead of giving a direct reply he said that my questions were moving away from the subject of the press conference. He used words which implied that I was using the press conference for my own agendas. I felt deeply disappointed and in the flow of my emotions took a step which shocked everyone. I did not have the intention of hurting Chidambaram. Despite my highly emotional state the shoe went towards a place where no one was sitting. It is a different story that a camera angle showed it in such a way that it seemed to be flying near the minister's face; in fact it was at least two to one and a half metres away.

Operation Blue Star, the 1984 massacre, the transistor bomb explosion in Delhi and terrorist attacks in Punjab on a daily basis, had spoiled the atmosphere. It is true I was young during that period, but my heart used to break whenever I heard of innocent people dying. If a person has harmed no one, then how can he or she be killed? I had read how Sikhs had fought against the atrocities of the Mughals, sacrificed their lives to fight British rule and showed their valour against the Chinese and Pakistanis in the 1962, 1965 and 1971 wars. How could the Sikhs be regarded as enemies of the country? Why did people have to connect the word 'Sikh' with 'terrorist'? After all, people did not talk of 'Muslim terrorists' or 'Hindu terrorists'. Those who killed Sikhs in the violence of 1984 were Hindus, so why are they not referred to as 'Hindu mobs'? When I would question my mother about terrorists killing innocents, she would say, 'A true Sikh cannot kill an innocent person. Those who are killing cannot be Sikhs.'

My mother's words ring true even today. The basis of Sikhs' beliefs is *Japuji Sahib* which states, 'Dhol Dharam Daya ka Poot.' Dharam is the son of compassion, meaning compassion is the basis of dharam and he who has none, cannot be a Sikh. When Guru Gobind Singh had wanted a Khalsa Panth (sect), Daya Singh had come forward. It cannot, to my mind, be a coincidence that the first to come was 'Daya' (compassion), then 'Dharam' (faith) Singh and then 'Himmat' (courage) Singh. Guru Gobind Singh tells us that when antagonism closes all roads and your enemies become determined to choose the path of violence, only then is it valid to fight them. It is permissible to raise a weapon to protect oneself; but to kill an innocent is a major act against dharam.

I had come from a gurdwara school to a government school in 1986 in class nine. I stood first in class eleven and I was to take the class twelve board examinations that year. The gurdwara school had a different atmosphere. At the government school one of the geography teachers would always address me as 'Listen, Sardar' instead of using my name. I had never heard such language in my earlier school. This sounded horrible. I used to wonder why the teacher couldn't call me by my name. But what can a lone student do? I was very good at geography but the teacher would never call on me to answer questions.

The same teacher ensured I received lower marks in my practicals, which meant I could not get a distinction in the subject though I had done well in my theory paper. I could not understand why the teacher was so unfair.

Despite no distinction in geography I got good marks in the class twelve board exam and I took admission in the nearby PGDAV College for a BA in political science. Cricket was my life and I had a good leg spin. The well-known cricketer from Indian Airlines, Ram Mohan, used to especially call me for spin practice. DAV College was the best college for cricket in Delhi. Ajay Sharma, Raman Lamba, Manoj Prabhakar, Atul Wasan, Maninder Singh, Manu Nayyar all had gone from the college team to the national team. I also started going to the cricket nets here. But the coach seemed to dislike me right from the beginning. My leg spin was very good—all the batsmen said so—but when I was not allowed to play a single practice match, I decided that it was better to concentrate on my studies.

During this time I would often discuss the Punjab situation, Sikhs and terrorism with my friends. I would tell them that a true Sikh can never kill an innocent person. Therefore, whoever kills an innocent cannot be a Sikh. Despite this my friend Sarvanand would jokingly ask, 'Hey terrorist, how are you?' But to be fair, he was not the only one: this feeling towards Sikhs was not unusual and an anti-Sikh atmosphere was building up. I would tell my friends about the peaceful teachings of the Sikh gurus and would not rest till I got them to agree with me. Whenever an argument on this subject took place, there was some souring in the relationship but otherwise the atmosphere was not bitter.

During this time I used to go to the Delhi Library near Chandni Chowk. When I saw the stacks of decades-old newspapers I immediately decided that I would see how the violence of 1984 had been reported. After searching for many hours, sifting through several heavy bundles of newspapers, it was saddening to note that the newspapers of those critical days seemed as if they were asleep. Except for the *Indian Express* and the Hindi language *Jan Satta* owned by the same group, there was nothing on the violence in other major publications. One could not make out from these newspapers that on 31 October and 1, 2 and 3 November, 3000 Sikhs had been killed in the national capital. Thousands of houses and shops had been burnt to ashes. *India Today* had some coverage, but after a month. There was no report on the massacre in the *Times of India* but there was an article written by journalist Girilal Jain which said, 'this is the result of the end of patience on the part of the Hindus'. Other national dailies also carried such articles. Why was this so? Why did the national print media, which independent, do this? Murders in Delhi are widely covered, why wasn't such a big massacre reported? I was puzzled: did some bias exist against the Sikhs in the media or was it because the media did not understand them? This was the reason I decided to become a journalist—they are part of society and they have information on what is happening. If I wanted to make an attempt to change this state of things, becoming a part of the media would be useful.

This was not easy. Right after graduation I had to earn a living. My family's economic status was not very secure and apart from my brother Gurcharan Bhai Sahib who had a job in a government-run organization, my three other brothers had just started in the car repairing business. Our situation was so uncertain that my younger brother had left his studies midway and had started working. The pressure was increasing on me too. People at home felt that if I started working instead of studying it would be better for all of us. Under these circumstances summer vacations were spent in lathe machine work or in learning AC work which my elder brother put me on to. For two months I worked hard at fixing car ACs, but I had not given up my dreams of becoming a journalist. Fortunately for me, because of Harshad Mehta's actions, the share market had begun to expand rapidly. Consequently, I found work for two months in a firm where I had to keep a record of the shareholders. Just to get breathing time and to do a course in journalism, I applied for an MA course to which I got admission but I discovered that there was an entrance test for the YMCA's course in journalism. I thought the test went well but when I went to see my results, my name was not on the list of successful candidates so I was really surprised when I was called for an interview—I could not believe it when I received the postcard inviting me to attend the interview. Till today I have not figured out how this happened. Truly it was destiny at work. When I went for the interview B.B. Nagpal from the UNI was the interviewer. He asked me a straight question on Punjab terrorism, 'Tell me, what is your opinion on Punjab terrorism?' I still remember my succinct, to-the-point answer, 'Demands and complaints can be valid, but a democratic form of protest should be employed. Violence is not the answer for this.' Perhaps Mr Nagpal liked my answer because I was admitted. I still wonder if he asked others this question too.

Becoming a journalist and establishing oneself is a difficult job. More so in Hindi journalism—the biases it is full of would make another book. Here it is sufficient to say that when the Nanavati Commission report came out in 2005 I wrote three articles on the subject, but my boss simply raised his hands helplessly. He said that he was being pressurized from the top. But he still raised his hands.

A shoe against injustice?

It was 12 August and the press gallery of the Rajya Sabha was full of activity. I had arrived early so that I could sit in the front row and not miss anything—every reporter worries about missing salient points. The Nanavati Commission report on the 1984 Sikh massacre had been presented in Parliament. Now it was for Prime Minister Manmohan Singh to explain the action to be taken on the basis of the report's recommendations. The then home minister Shivraj Patil kept a bundle of action reports in front of him but this was nothing more than form filling. When the prime minister came to Parliament he was looking a little emotional but otherwise composed. In fact by then the minister of state for non-resident Indian affairs, Jagdish Tytler, had already agreed to resign as minister of state the Nanavati Commission had recommended a fresh probe against him. The Nanavati Commission report brought to light strong evidence against Sajjan Kumar and Tytler in the violence of 1984.

Furthermore, the commission had strongly recommended restarting investigations into the charges against them. In this situation if Tytler had continued to be a member of the cabinet, it would have been an embarrassment for the government. Before the Opposition asked for his resignation, the government had decided to distance itself. When the prime minister started speaking, the entire House as well as journalists in the press gallery listened carefully to each word. He took the help of a few words from the Guruvani (words of the Guru) and highlighted the Sikh community's service to the country—how the Sikhs had been at the forefront of the fight against injustice from the struggle for independence to Partition. And, despite bearing the brunt of Partition, they had moved ahead. The prime minister's words, putting the contribution of the Sikhs into perspective before the nation, were very encouraging.

Then he came to the Nanavati Commission report and said that action would be taken on the basis of its recommendations. The CBI would investigate and no accused person against whom charges were proved would be allowed to go free. The relief package for the victims was to be increased and the payments would be done in a given period of time. He also talked about the Nanavati Commission giving a clean chit to the then High

Command. I didn't like that but then the prime minister said, 'Whatever happened with the Sikhs in 1984 is a big blot on the forehead of the country and my head hangs in shame for this.' He apologized to the Sikhs on behalf of the government and the country. The prime minister concluded, 'We cannot rewrite history but we can make the future better.' After this speech, there was little the Opposition could add. In the press gallery the reporters agreed that the kind of speech Manmohan Singh had made that day was unprecedented. The speech was unique and it also was a balm to the wounded hearts of the Sikhs. The prime minister had expressed his sadness in the country's Parliament. Now he was asking the Sikhs to leave this black chapter behind and move forward. Together with this he had given his word that the CBI would undertake investigations against the accused with full sincerity.

While I filed the report I felt as if a big burden had been lifted. I had a happy feeling in my heart. The point was not that Manmohan Singh was a Sikh; the point was that the prime minister of the country had at last expressed regret for the massacre of Sikhs. Compare this to the situation in 1984 when Parliament—which can come to a halt even over a small scandal—did not discuss the orchestrated violence against the Sikh community in the capital of the country.

In the 1984 Lok Sabha elections the Congress won 404 seats out of the total of 545. The BJP got only two. The leader of the Opposition had been selected from the Communist Party of India (Marxist) (CPI[M]) because the party had won twenty-two seats. The CPI(M) which prides itself on being the flag bearer of secularism and has consistently championed the rights of the Muslim minority, has displayed little concern over the suffering of the Sikhs. I have great respect for their sensitive attitude towards labour, the backward sections and the poor, but I cannot understand their attitude towards the Sikh community. If they are allergic to religion, then why do they have sympathy for some religious minorities and not for others? Whatever the reasons, the eighth Lok Sabha did not discuss the anti-Sikh violence that had engulfed the capital. The fifteenth Lok Sabha redeemed this and created history thanks to Prime Minister Manmohan Singh.

Subsequently, however, while the government has shown its seriousness in addressing the issue of compensation for the victims of the 1984 violence, the CBI continues to procrastinate on its investigation.

In 1999 when the Congress Party president Sonia Gandhi went to Darbar Sahib in Amritsar to pay her respects, she said, 'Events like 1984 should never happen again, we are entering a new millennium, let us do so in a spirit of forgiveness.' The message was clear that she wanted to improve her relationship with the Sikhs and Punjab. In the following Punjab assembly elections, Captain Amarinder Singh, who had left the Congress after Operation Blue Star, was made the chief ministerial candidate. Sonia Gandhi's spotless image and honesty had begun to have its effect on the Sikhs. Besides this, the faith she clearly showed in Dr Manmohan Singh's prime ministership after the 2004 Lok Sabha elections was a source of pride for the community as a whole. These steps by Sonia Gandhi and the Congress were reinforced by the visit of Rahul Gandhi to Punjab in September 2008. The tour was meant to connect with the youth of Punjab but during this time he took concrete steps to remove the bitterness of the past. At a press conference in Amritsar, his answer to a question was, 'The 1984 riots were wrong and I strongly condemn the carnage.' This gave the feeling that he was serious.

I, too, felt he was serious, so my disappointment was greater when, on his return to Delhi, he was photographed with the two men accused of being the main perpetrators of the violence—Sajjan Kumar and Jagdish Tytler. The Sikh Forum which had welcomed Rahul Gandhi's speech a day before, expressed its regret at the photograph the very next day. Efforts were being made to address the pain of the

Sikhs in speeches, but political will in taking action against the accused was less apparent. The main focus seemed to be to give the Sikhs compensation and to urge them to forget the massacre. This was seriously underestimating the depth of the outrage within the Sikh community.

Even in the case against Jagdish Tytler, it was only when the court reprimanded the CBI that an official went and took the statement of witness Jasbir Singh in America—the CBI had persisted in maintaining it had not been able to trace the witness. It took five years to challenge the acquittal of Sajjan Kumar. Despite recommendations by the Nanavati Commission, the government refused to act against the accused police officers on the grounds that they had either retired or because it was not possible to take action against them after so long a period. The feeling in the Sikh community was that had the government wanted to, it could have found a way. Or it could have at least expressed its views so forcibly on the police actions in 1984 that the present police structure could take a lesson from that. This did not happen. In the meantime, in January 2009, when the matter concerning Harcharan Singh Josh with respect to 1984 came to the high court, the court observed that the wounds of 1984 had healed, therefore there was no point in trying to stretch the matter any further.

This comment was a source of deep hurt to the Sikh community. In a situation where the first FIR was filed after eleven years, where witnesses have been threatened and bribed into changing their statements—actions which made a mockery of law—the talk of wounds having healed was offensive. The victims of the 1984 violence were not asking for charity. Was the demand for justice or even the expectation of it, a crime? All this disturbed me. In the meantime on 18 February that year in Mohali, Punjab, another witness, Gurcharan Singh, died. He had been bedridden since he was injured in 1984 and was the main witness against Sajjan Kumar. Anek Kaur, another major witness against Sajjan Kumar, had died several years before. Now the witnesses were all passing away but the wheel of the law was not ready to turn. The promises of punishing the accused that had been made on the floor of Parliament were fast vanishing.

The Congress had given Sajjan Kumar and Jagdish Tytler Lok Sabha tickets. The Sikh community has always regarded giving tickets to the accused in the 1984 massacre as a slap on its face. After all Sonia Gandhi had called Narendra Modi and his government 'maut ke saudagar' (traders of death) because of their actions during the attacks on Muslims in Gujarat; yet two of the main accused in the 1984 violence were candidates of the party. Sajjan Kumar and Jagdish Tytler have been the accused in every commission and committee that has investigated the violence. The worst blow fell when, just before the elections, the CBI recommended that all cases against Jagdish Tytler be closed. I remember my friends in the bureau condemned it wholeheartedly, calling it a shameless act, maintaining that the CBI would never have closed such a high-profile case without instructions from the very top. The CBI's reasons were that it did not have faith in the witnesses. Was the CBI now a court? Its job is to investigate, not judge whether the witnesses are reliable. It knew that many witnesses had been intimidated into withdrawing their statements against the powerful; those who had shown the courage to persist were being dismissed without reason. One of the last rays of hope for justice was going. On 2 April 2009, asked about the clean chit to the accused, the home minister, P. Chidambaram said, 'I am happy that my friend has been acquitted by the CBI.' What kind of message was he giving to investigative agencies and government machinery. This was the country's home minister who had won the country's respect for the tough line he took after the heinous terrorist attack in Mumbai on 26 November 2008.

The Congress-led UPA's victory in the 2009 Lok Sabha elections was perhaps due in no little part to the fact that there had been no terrorist attacks since. This had effectively blunted the edge of the BJP's stance that the Congress was soft on terror. Many journalists have observed that Chidambaram is amongst the most capable political leaders today. His unflappable manner, his undoubted intelligence, his measured speech, all bear out this assessment. But how could he think that the victims who had waited for justice for twenty-five years would not be appalled by the CBI's position.

I was deeply disturbed. My main beat was defence but because of the imminent Lok Sabha polls, from February 2009 the entire bureau was asked to concentrate on the elections. For the special news page it was mandatory to give three news items connected with the elections every week. My beat was Punjab, Himachal Pradesh and Jammu and Kashmir and it was my responsibility to report on the Congress Party's ticket distribution and political strategies for these areas. The Election Commission had long been my beat and violations in the model election code of conduct were extensively covered. During this time, the Rajasthan unit of the BJP registered a complaint against the home minister for using an official tour as an election tour. The Election Commission took this act as a first-degree violation of the election code and sent him a notice. Chidambaram was asked to respond by 6 April.

The minister was returning to Delhi on 6 April itself and had to give an answer the same day. He called a press conference at noon at the Congress headquarters. As my newspaper's weekly meeting was to be held at the same time, I was not planning to attend, but it was postponed to 7 April. I had no assignment that day and so I decided to attend to get some news of his reply to the Election Commission, and since I was going, I decided to ask Chidambaram about the 1984 cases. There was a hearing in the court regarding this case the very next day.

I remember that I was eager to ask a question and raised my hand right from the beginning, but my turn came after eight to ten questions. I had been waiting for this moment for a long time. I first congratulated him on the formation of the National Investigation Agency (NIA) and other important steps he had taken after the Mumbai bomb explosions. But the question I really wanted to ask was different and so close to my heart that I started getting emotional. Perhaps all the pain from a long time had come together at this point. I asked, if rioters are 'maut ke saudagar' in Gujarat, then how could he, the home minister, be happy at the clean chit given to Tytler? He gave a technical answer but when I tried to ask a follow-up question he said this was not a matter for this press conference. Chidambaram's reply was—'The case is sub judice'. I asked if Tytler's case was not being taken on as part of a strategy. Instead of giving a direct reply he implied I was using the press conference for my own agendas. I took a step which shocked everyone. I did not have the intention of hurting Chidambaram. Despite my extreme emotion the shoe went towards a place where nobody was sitting even though a camera angle showed it in such a way as if it went near his face. I then sat down.

I accept this action was a violation of the codes of journalism but the issue I have raised was just. Later, when I was asked I expressed my regret as a journalist at the incident but also said that those people who have done the injustice should actually be the ones to apologize. For the past twenty-five years the police have violated their codes, their ethics. Instead of saving people, they allowed them to be killed and then did not register cases against the killers. The people in power, instead of letting justice take its course, made the accused ministers. All these people had violated their codes for twenty-five years. To remind them of their 'ethics' a journalist had violated his 'ethics', yes, but I also wanted to remind the entire system of its insensitivity to and its responsibility for the continuing injustice. I have no regrets for raising this grave injustice.

All the journalists were shocked. How had the quiet Jarnail Singh done this?

The security personnel immediately took me out of the room. As we were emerging from the Congress headquarters, the television crews surrounded us. I immediately said I accepted this was a violation of ethics as a journalist, but what about the people who had not accepted their mistakes for the past twenty-five years? I had no regrets. This was an 'Unprecedented Protest' against 'Unprecedented Injustice'; it was not against Chidambaram personally.

I was taken to the Tughlak Road police station. The questioning began as soon as I reached there. All agencies including the Intelligence Bureau (IB) came to question me and all this went on for about half an hour. They asked me my telephone numbers and had them locked immediately. My journalist's Press Information Bureau (PIB) card was also taken from me. I was questioned about each member of my family and I answered to the best of my ability. While this was going on, instructions reached the police station that no case was to be registered against me. However, I was not told anything about this. At that point my colleague, Sanjay Mishra, came in and the police said they were taking me to another location. Sanjay came along in the police jeep. Shortly after that the jeep abruptly returned to the police station. I was told I was free and I left in Sanjay's car. The media had collected outside the station. I talked about the sacrifices of the Sikhs for the country and repeated that the subject was correct even if the means of protest was not. Sanjay advised me not to say anything, but I felt the situation should be clear and that is why I said what I did. We had gone a little way in the police jeep when I was brought back to the police station and made to sit in Sanjay's car. Sanjay told me that no case was being registered against me and that Chidambaram himself had said this. When the journalist inside me made an evaluation of this, I realized that looking at the sensitive nature of the subject, this was the right decision. Next day Chidambaram in an interview to a TV channel had said, 'I understand the pain of the Sikhs. Not many people have been punished in the riots.'

Sanjay wanted to keep me away from the media. He is amongst my best friends but I could not listen to what he said. On the way Sanjay realized that the media would have also reached my house. Therefore, he took me to his house. It was not pleasant to watch myself throw the shoe again and again on television. I wondered why the media, instead of focusing on the 1984 issue, was giving so much importance to the shoe-throwing.

I stayed at Sanjay's place and had lunch there. I had not switched on my cellphone at his request. But realized that would have to face the media eventually and it was important to focus on the massacre of 1984. I told Sanjay to drop me off at my brother's house. By this time I came to know that the people involved in Sikh politics as well as others had started to gather at my house. Not finding me there, the media was talking to my family at home. I has apprehensive: I know the television media very well and was worried that they might try and put words into the mouths of my family who had no experience of the camera or the press. I instructed all the people at home to not say anything to the media.

When I switched on my phone to call up home there were several missed calls and SMSs. One was from Rajdeep Sardesai, the head of CNN-IBN, which said that the Editor's Guild was going to make a statement condemning my action, and I should, therefore, speak to them first and clarify my position. I felt that I should clarify things. When I called back he said that they were sending a cameraperson and that I should express my point of view. I could not refuse, but since I was giving a statement to CNN-IBN I decided to reply to NDTV 24×7's Barkha Dutt's SMS as well and quietly asked them to send in their cameraperson too. To the cameras I repeated that as a journalist I regretted what had happened but that the subject was perfectly valid.

Till now I had not known that on that very day, the Akali Dal (Badal) had also decided to stage a dharna at

Jantar Mantar. This was covered by our local office so that is why I had no information on it. When a journalist asked me about my protest and the Akali Dal procession taking place on the same day, I said, 'Would the home minister P. Chidambaram and the Akali Dal get together and fix the same day?' In the meantime, indications started coming from the Congress that it would reconsider the nominations of Jagdish Tytler and Sajjan Kumar. The media here and abroad had highlighted this incident, and by now—for the first time in twenty-five years—they had also moved on from just reporting the shoe-throwing to covering the violence of 1984. Besides my violations of journalistic ethics, the Congress had no answer on this subject. Also, Dr Manmohan Singh had to be projected as the prime minister and the Lok Sabha elections were around the corner.

I have a feeling that a part of the Congress felt that whatever happened in 1984 should not reach the top leadership and that is why the entire topic was being kept under wraps. The Congress did not want to talk about 1984. Even so, when it would try to corner the BJP on the Gujarat riots the Opposition would remind it of the 1984 riots. It bothers me as to what extent it is acceptable to protest one instance of injustice by reminding others of the injustice they have committed. Both are leading political parties; instead of blaming each other, why don't they get together to remove the roots of communalism?

After the shoe-throwing incident

In the meantime, while some political parties announced a Lok Sabha ticket for me, others lined up money and honours. Yet another one was ready to buy my shoe for Rs 5 lakh and another promised me lakhs of rupees. I had expressed the sentiments of the Sikhs. Why were these people putting a price on my emotions? Why were they throwing political dirt?

I had to say some strong words about this to the media to clarify doubts which were being deliberately raised against me. The way I was being presented was far from the truth. The very next day was the hearing of the Tytler case in court. The protest processions were getting more vehement and pressure on the Congress was increasing. The Congress was hoping to do well in Punjab and media coverage was such that the state Congress leaders started saying that the Sajjan Kumar and Jagdish Tytler cases were having an adverse effect on the elections there. The truth is that the facts had not changed; but the Congress had ignored the facts when allotting tickets. When Captain Amarinder Singh was asked about the clear chit given to Tytler, he said that the 1984 riots are a non-issue for the Sikhs. But after the shoe had been thrown the media took the view that the Punjab Congress was also putting pressure on the Congress leadership not to give tickets to the accused men. The Congress waited for the ruling of the court next day and when the court announced another date for hearing, they also got the feeling that it was time to wipe this blot away to some extent. Had they not done this it would have been an issue throughout the entire election campaign. Especially when a Sikh was being projected as prime minister, it was difficult to keep this subject under wraps. The Congress leadership realized—even if due to the 'Unprecedented Protest'—that the pain of 1984 is very deep and the Sikhs would not forget. The result came to the forefront in the evening press conference of Jagdish Tytler who talked about giving up his nomination. The prime minister was speaking at the Indian Women's Press Corps. When asked about the withdrawal of the ticket he endorsed my protest by saying, '*Der aayad durust aayad*' meaning it has come late but it is correct. I did not feel like a victor, but I was definitely relieved. The prime minister said that he wasn't aware that Jagdish Tytler had been given a clean chit.

After the incident I received many invitations to speak at or participate in various functions. It was election time and being a journalist I could assess the motives behind many of them. I had to think clearly about the political colour that could be given to even innocent actions. I only participated in programmes which I felt were worthwhile. For instance, I joined in a rally against alcoholism and drug abuse held in Makbulpura, Amritsar. This had the added attraction allowing me to pay my respects and thank God at the Darbar Sahib.

The SGPC told me that I would be presented with a siropa, a ceremonial scarf, during my visit. I was upset as I had taken care to ensure that no one could accuse me of exploiting the incident, but my journalist friends said accepting a siropa was not giving out a political message. To refuse would be very ungracious. The committee's president, Awtar Singh Makkad, presented me with the siropa and offered me the post of the SGPC's media adviser. I refused. I did not want to be a part of any political faction. But I will never forget the appreciation that I have received from ordinary Sikhs at the Darbar Sahib. A Sikh lady, hearing I was there, ran barefoot for nearly a kilometre behind my rickshaw—I cannot express how much I was moved. Youngsters who had not even been born in 1984 wanted to get their photographs clicked with me. I heard the Daadhi (bearded) Sikhs, who sing about history in a special style, telling the story of how

I threw the shoe in their Vaar singing in the hallowed halls of Manji Sahib in the Harmandir Sahib precincts. I felt as if God had blessed me.

I was happiest when the widows who had been victims of the riots expressed satisfaction at the withdrawal of election tickets to both Sajjan Kumar and Jagdish Tytler. And when I was presented the siropa in the widows' colony gurdwara, it was the most satisfying day of my life.

A number of other shoe-throwing incidents took place soon after, but I feel they were mostly for personal or political gains.

On election day, I refused to vote even though I had been covering the Election Commission for a long time, giving special importance to their appeals for a higher voter turnout. However, this time I felt that there was no candidate or party that could be called truly secular and therefore I did not vote. Nonetheless I was happy that Manmohan Singh became the prime minister again.

After the shoe-throwing incident I had been asked by my newspaper office not to attend office for twenty days. They had also advised me not to speak to the media. After twenty days when I asked if I should return to work, I was told to wait till the elections were over.

After thwarting all attempts at being pressured to resign I was officially fired on 1 July 2009. I want to mention here that despite having lost my job, my journalist friends have stood by me: Saikat Dutta from *Outlook*, Sandeep Dixit from *The Hindu* and Gautam Dutt from the *Indian Express* who came to the Tughlak Road police station at the time of the incident. Their support was heartening. Sujan Dutta's piece in the *Telegraph*, 'Byline to Headline: an emotionally overtaken Sardar reveals his hurt', was touching. Hartosh Bal also wrote a fantastic article. *Tehelka* magazine gave me support and seasoned journalists like Harinder Baweja, Vir Sanghvi and Kanwar Sandhu supported me for raising the issue. This was a source of great comfort. Bharat Bhushan, the editor of *Mail Today*, gave me the chance to clarify my position after I had lost my job. I feel that since I had accepted that I had violated journalistic ethics, the media community understood my action.

In the end, whatever the actual events behind the rescinding of tickets to Jagdish Tytler and Sajjan Kumar were, the consequence, as the *World Sikh News* wrote in the second week of April, was that the wheel of law, which had not turned for the past twenty-five years, was turned by a shoe travelling a distance of one and a half metres.

I was happiest when the widows who had been victims of the riots expressed satisfaction at the withdrawal of election tickets to both Sajjan Kumar and Jagdish Tytler. And when I was presented the siropa in the widows' colony gurdwara, it was the most satisfying day of my life.

A number of other shoe-throwing incidents took place soon after, but I feel they were mostly for personal or political gains.

On election day, I refused to vote even though I had been covering the Election Commission for a long time, giving special importance to their appeals for a higher voter turnout. However, this time I felt that there was no candidate or party that could be called truly secular and therefore I did not vote. Nonetheless I was happy that Manmohan Singh became the prime minister again.

After the shoe-throwing incident I had been asked by my newspaper office not to attend office for twenty days. They had also advised me not to speak to the media. After twenty days when I asked if I should return to work, I was told to wait till the elections were over.

After thwarting all attempts at being pressured to resign I was officially fired on 1 July 2009. I want to mention here that despite having lost my job, my journalist friends have stood by me: Saket Dutta from *Outlook*, Sandeep Dixit from *The Hindu* and Gautam Dutt from the *Indian*

Express who came to the Tughlak Road police station at the time of the incident. Their support was heartening. Sujan Dutta's piece in the *Telegraph*, 'Byline to Headline: an emotionally overtaken Sardar reveals his hurt', was touching. Hartosh Bal also wrote a fantastic article. *Tehelka* magazine gave me support and seasoned journalists like Harinder Baweja, Vir Sanghvi and Kavinder Sandhu supported me for raising the issue. This was a source of great comfort. Bharat Bhushan, the editor of *Mail Today*, gave me the chance to clarify my position after I had lost my job. I feel that since I had accepted that I had violated journalistic ethics, the media community understood my action.

In the end, whatever the actual events behind the rescinding of tickets to Jagdish Tytler and Sajjan Kumar were, the consequence, as the *World Sikh News* wrote in the second week of April, was that the wheel of law, which had not turned for the past twenty-five years, was turned by a shoe travelling a distance of one and a half metres.